"James Ishmael Ford sets forth his richly informative account of the history and nature of the Zen koan. He also provides us with a beautifully nuanced account of how to introspect a koan and the transformation that occurs over time with such work. Ford brings his long and extensive experience as a Zen teacher to encourage and inspire us to take up the koan path and to discover the boundless in the midst of our daily activity. In so doing he doesn't shirk the challenges and pitfalls that arise in the course of the journey. What shines through everywhere in this inspiring book is Ford's humanity, his love of teaching, and his honesty and compassion. *Introduction to Zen Koans* provides the reader with a comprehensive account of the Zen Way with the koan at its heart. Properly, Ford gives emphasis to the fact that Silent Illumination and koan introspection are complementary paths, and that students, regardless of the tradition in which they train, should travel both. In so doing Ford heals ancient sectarian divisions and sets forth an appropriate path for Zen practitioners in the twenty-first century. This is a much-needed book—one that will invite, challenge, and inspire you. As you learn the language of dragons, you transform your life."

—ROSS BOLLETER, author of
*The Crow Flies Backwards and Other New Zen Koans*

INTRODUCTION TO

# ZEN KOANS

## Learning the Language of Dragons

JAMES ISHMAEL FORD

Foreword by Joan Halifax

Wisdom Publications
199 Elm Street
Somerville, MA 02144 USA
wisdompubs.org

*Library of Congress Cataloging-in-Publication Data*
Names: Ford, James Ishmael, author. | Halifax, Joan, writer of foreword.
Title: Introduction to Zen koans: learning the language of dragons / James Ishmael Ford;
    foreword by Joan Halifax.
Description: Somerville, MA: Wisdom Publications, 2018. | Includes bibliographical
    references. |
Identifiers: LCCN 2017037686 (print) | LCCN 2017039295 (ebook) | ISBN 9781614293156
    (ebook) | ISBN 9781614292951 (pbk.: alk. paper)
Subjects: LCSH: Koan.
Classification: LCC BQ9289.5 (ebook) | LCC BQ9289.5 .F67 2018 (print) | DDC
    294.3/85—dc23
LC record available at https://lccn.loc.gov/2017037686

ISBN 978-1-61429-295-1    ebook ISBN 978-1-61429-315-6
22 21 20 19 18        5  4  3  2  1

Cover design by Phil Pascuzzo. Cover artwork by Jan Zaremba. Set in Arno Pro 10.9/15.

Wisdom Publications' books are printed on acid-free paper and meet the guidelines
for permanence and durability of the Production Guidelines for Book Longevity
of the Council on Library Resources.

✿ This book was produced with environmental mindfulness.
For more information, please visit wisdompubs.org/
wisdom-environment.

Printed in the United States of America.

For Julia Bernard, who loved dragons,

and Jan Seymour-Ford, who knows their language

# Contents

## PART THREE: Living Zen

# Foreword

THIS MARVELOUS BOOK opens the treasure house of Zen and yet, happily, does not dispel its mystery. Roshi James Ford, an excellent storyteller and longtime Zen practitioner and teacher, presents a detailed and beautiful description of the craft of zazen, including "just sitting" and various forms of breath meditation—but focuses primarily on koan introspection.

The power of koans, these "public cases" from China, has never ceased to enrich my experience of Zen. They are a medium of exploration of the history, culture, and view of Zen, but most importantly they are a medium of awakening.

Roshi Ford is fundamentally a koan person, and for this, the book is particularly rich, opening the practice of koans in a splendid way. I am grateful for his long experience as a teacher and practitioner of this rare and powerful practice. Since the word *koan* has found its way into popular English usage, I am grateful too for the more nuanced and fertile view of koans that Ford presents. His definition of the word is telling: "a koan points to something of deep importance and invites us to stand in that place."

He has also created a wonderful translation of the Heart Sutra, Zen's central scripture—and carefully opens up the heart of the Heart Sutra through scholarship and practice. Rich in textual sources and woven throughout with the perspectives of contemporary teachers, *Introduction to Zen Koans* sheds new light on ancient teachings. Through it, the reader will discover the importance of lineage, the traceless traces of the Zen ancestors, and the places of "just sitting" and koan practice as paths to awakening, as the great doorways into Zen.

ROSHI JOAN HALIFAX, PHD, is a Buddhist teacher, Zen priest, anthropologist, and pioneer in the field of end-of-life care. The author of *Being with Dying* and *The Fruitful Darkness,* she is the head teacher of Upaya Zen Center, a founding teacher of the Zen Peacemaker Order, and founder of Prajna Mountain Buddhist Order.

# PROLOGUE

## *Encountering the Language of Dragons*

THERE IS A STORY about a man in ancient China who loved dragons. Unlike dragons in Western culture, who guard hoards of treasure and menace maidens and villages, dragons in China, while dangerous, are also carriers of great wisdom. In the Zen Way, they're often used as a symbol for our deepest wisdom. In this story, the man was fascinated with the idea of dragons. He studied them, collected art objects that featured them, and even dreamed about them.

Somehow the king of dragons heard of this man and decided to reward him with a visit. He thought he could tutor the man in the language of dragons, the language of ultimate reality. When he arrived the man was asleep in his bed. And so the dragon settled itself at the foot of his bed, curling its long tail and sitting quietly. When the man awoke and saw the dragon he was terrified. He grabbed a sword and waved it at the king of the dragons.

Disappointed, the dragon flew up and returned to the mysteries.

PRESUMABLY, if you've opened this book, you have an interest in Zen and its practices. And the language of Zen is the language of dragons. This book is about learning that language. It is essentially a meditation manual that explores three things. The first thing is Zen's meditation disciplines. The second thing is an understanding of the great insight that lies at the heart of those disciplines, like that curled dragon. And the third thing is the way in which Zen's meditation disciplines are part of a larger context of practice, a great Middle Way, which is ignored at some peril. Think of these as the various parts of the grammar of this language of the wise heart. They each inform the other and give us the Zen Way.

Mastering this language isn't easy. In fact, it can be disturbing, on occasion even terrifying, to open ourselves as fully as this Way does. These practices reveal treasures. And they reveal secrets. Sometimes these secrets too are terribly painful. So there are perhaps good reasons that man who loved dragons in the abstract found their reality so distressing. After all, Zen deals with the fundamental matters of our human hearts, and, while powerful and transformative, Zen as a way of life also plays rough with our ideas of who and what we are.

That's the language of dragons.

PART ONE

# The Heart of Zen

# 1

# Buddha Means *Awake*

SOME FOUR OR FIVE OR SIX centuries before the birth of Jesus, there was a remarkable sage. His name was Gautama Siddhartha. His story is one of the great tales of the world's spirituality.

Long ago, a queen named Love learned she was pregnant. The king called together his astrologers and wise ones, and asked them to chart out the fate of this princeling.

They conferred with the stars and ancient texts. The queen told them that she first knew she was pregnant when she dreamed that four *devas*, celestial beings, escorted her to a hidden valley, and brought her to the edge of a limpid pool of water.

The devas bathed her, gave her clothing even more beautiful than her own, sprinkled perfume on her, and braided flowers into her hair. As she stood there, a great white elephant holding a lotus flower in its trunk came to her, circled around her three times, and then magically walked into her right side.

Taking all this information into account, the council went to the king with their prognostication. There was no doubt, they told him, that this was to be a remarkable child, unprecedented in the history of the world. But there were two paths this child might grow up to walk. The first was to become the greatest warrior-king the world had ever witnessed, unifying all countries under a single banner.

The second was to become a sage, a teacher of a way unspoken of before. He would unfold a path that would offer liberation from the common bondage of human hurt, a path to the true healing of the human heart. In short, following that second path, the child could become the greatest spiritual teacher in the world's history.

Hoping for the first option and dreading the second, the king decided the only way to guide his child to worldly success would be to isolate him from anything that might spark the spiritual quest. And so he created a pleasure palace where the child would be raised to ride and fight and never be confronted with the sadnesses of human life.

Subsequently, the young Siddhartha grew into manhood, strong and able—and completely unaware of what the world was really like. At the appropriate time he was presented with a beautiful wife. They had a child. It seemed his joy was unmatchable—but at the same time he felt haunted. He knew he was isolated. He knew something existed beyond those walls marking the boundaries of his life.

One evening, accompanied by a single faithful servant, he sneaked out into the city. There he witnessed three things: he saw a dreadfully sick person, he witnessed old age for the first time, and he saw a corpse. He was shocked each time to learn that these things were the common fate of humanity. Finally he saw one more striking thing: a mendicant, clothed in rags, and sitting in silent meditation. And that person seemed to radiate peacefulness.

Haunted by these sights, the young prince returned to the palace. Those scenes would not leave his dreams and would rise unbidden at the strangest times during the day. Finally he determined he had to deal with the issue. Again, one evening he sneaked out of the palace, and, at the gate to the city, he exchanged his royal finery for a peasant's rags.

He undertook years of spiritual discipline. Knowing he needed some guidance, he met and submitted to two of the great spiritual teachers at that time. The first was Alara Kalama, a yogi and meditation teacher who guided him to some experience of emptiness. Eventually the teacher declared he had nothing more to teach the young monk and offered to share the teacher's seat with him. Not yet feeling the peace he sought, Siddhartha left.

His next teacher was Uddaka Ramaputta, another yogi and also a meditation teacher. That man initiated Siddhartha into the realms of "immaterial" attainments, realms of mental activity so subtle they seem unconnected to the body. After some time, again, he was told that he had achieved all that the teacher had to give—and was offered a shared place on the teacher's seat. Knowing he had not yet won the great victory, he again decided to continue on his way.

Siddhartha then embarked on a path of extreme privation. It's said that for a time he survived on a single grain of rice a day. Even as he grew more and more emaciated, his persistence attracted other seekers, and soon he had five companions, each striving harder and harder to separate themselves from the clinging of the body. This went on for years.

Siddhartha finally decided this too was a failed way. All it brought was more suffering. And so he eventually accepted a bowl of gruel from a young girl and drank from a stream. When his companions saw this, they were appalled that he would succumb to the urges of the body, and they left him.

Siddhartha reflected. As a child, he had had a great intimation; it was much like the experiences he had with his meditation teachers. What if he didn't simply stop at those experiences of deep peace, as his former teachers counseled? What if he went further on, witnessing whatever happened? What might he find?

Now alone, he settled himself under the shade of a tree, sat upright, and quieted himself as he had been taught—but then continued, looking. Just watching, just witnessing.

The forces of delusion saw the time was at hand, a new age was birthing, and these forces did all they could to stop the former prince bringing the way of wisdom into the world. The chief of these was Mara. Mara threw before his gaze dreams of Siddhartha's old life, his family, the offers of kingship and guru status. His fears in life were paraded in front of him. His longings were put on full display.

But Siddhartha continued watching, continued witnessing. Later there were moments of extreme bliss. Joy washed over him—and he continued watching. For forty days and forty nights he sat. Perhaps he slept a little, but he never lay down. He continued watching. And then it happened. One early morning, as Venus rose in the sky, he looked up at it—and he *knew*. He sang out to the world, "Oh, I see! The world and I awaken together."

Yet, as is the fact with real awakening, our troubles do not end upon seeing this. The tempter tried one more time, whispering in Siddhartha's ear, "You have won your liberation from the endless cycle of hurt! Now retire from the world and enjoy the bliss of eternity for the rest of your life, and then enter into the final peace."

Instead, though, Siddhartha thought of his family and of the suffering world, and he got up and started looking for his former companions. As he walked down the path a sage saw him and his strange countenance, something the sage had never witnessed before. He said to Siddhartha, "Who are you? A god?"

Siddhartha said, "No."

"Then perhaps a deva?"

"No."

Knowing this was no ordinary person, the sage persisted. "What are you?"

And Siddhartha said, "I am awake."

"Buddha" means *awake*.

HE SPENT forty years preaching his awakened wisdom. His teachings have been described in a number of ways. The most famous is as the four noble truths. These were captured in two separate texts that purport to transmit his direct teachings. The four truths, using Sanskrit terms, are *dukkha*, *samudaya*, *nirodha*, and *marga*.

*Dukkha* is our human suffering, anguish, angst. It is the sorrow that haunts human existence. It is not having what we want, and not wanting what we have. It is that pervasive sense of disease that shadows human life, and more broadly the tension of all existence.

*Samudaya* is the observation that we are composed of parts in constant motion. While even the "parts" are in fact insubstantial, our human minds perceive this motion as if it were solid. When we try to hold on tightly to that which is constantly changing we experience dukkha.

*Nirodha* is Buddhism's good news. It means "cessation"—and means we need not suffer this way.

*Marga* is the Middle Way, or eightfold path of liberation. These are right, correct, profitable "view," "resolve," "speech," "conduct," "livelihood," "effort," "mindfulness," and "concentration." Even in his lifetime people found it helpful to simplify this list. His disciple the nun Dhammadinna divided these eight aspects into three parts that make up the Buddha's Way: wisdom, morality, and meditation.

There is another categorization of his teachings that I've also found helpful. It is a way of seeing into our lives, our hurt, and our healing through the "three marks of existence." The first of these is called in Sanskrit *anitya*, a noticing that all things are impermanent, existing for a moment and then passing away.

The second is *anatman*, the noticing that nothing has a special essence. All things are composed of parts that are themselves insubstantial, or perhaps more accurately, have no abiding substance. Things exist within their moments in ways perhaps similar to the contemporary wave/particle theory, where from one angle quantum entities are particles and from another waves.

The third mark is *dukkha*, where our grasping tightly after things that have no enduring substance leads to that sense of discomfort, of sadness, of hurt that seems to mark our human existence.

People resonated with his teachings.

They adapted them to their own lives.

And then they shared them with others.

Very quickly Buddhism became a missionary religion with that good news to share, the possibility of liberation from suffering. Because of this, monks, nuns, merchants, and miscellaneous others began, from near the beginning of its formation, to carry Buddhism's teachings to others near and far.

With each encounter things happened. There were changes in orientation, changes of focus, clarifications, and occasionally whole new variations on this now ancient Way. Among these encounters perhaps the most dramatic was when Indian Buddhism came to China.

2

# Zen's Two Stories

IN CLASSICAL CHINA, a civilization with an ancient culture and worldviews, two new stories emerge that are critical to understanding Zen. These new stories were not so different than the story of the Awakened One, the Buddha, Gautama Siddhartha, that Indian prince who discovered some great secrets of the human heart. But they're not the same story, either.

The first of Zen's stories tells of another Indian prince who became a monk in a line of transmission that went directly back twenty-eight generations to the Buddha. Sometime early in the sixth century, this Indian prince decided to bring the Great Way to China. His name was Bodhidharma. He undertook the indignities, difficulties, and dangers of traveling the Silk Road. Finally he made his way to the Chinese imperial capital.

Bodhidharma was granted an interview with Emperor Wu of Liang. The emperor was a great supporter of the forms of Buddhism that had already migrated to China. Out of his embracing of the Way he prohibited animal sacrifice and abolished capital punishment except for the most extreme crimes. He had even done a little suppressing of Daoism as a rival tradition. But mostly, his work was positive. Emperor Wu founded universities, expanded access to the Confucian civil service exam, and endowed monasteries and convents. The emperor was excited at the prospect of an encounter with such an eminent monk. When finally they came face to face, the emperor launched into a list of his good deeds in support of the Buddha's Way. It was a long list indeed.

The emperor then asked if the venerable monk had an opinion about the merit the emperor generated through these many acts. The emperor was profoundly concerned with evil karma, its consequences, and how to dissipate its negative effects. His wife, Empress Chi, had recently died, and he had learned through diviners that she was suffering torments in the hell realms on account of her obsessive anger in life.

He commissioned a text, known as *Emperor Liang's Jeweled Repentance,* and an accompanying ceremony to save her and others from the hell realms. And this wasn't his only brush with the matter of karma and its expiation. There was an even more intimate reason. Through misunderstandings, the emperor himself had unknowingly ordered the execution of a famous monk, and his guilt and anxiety continued to haunt him. He was obsessed with the problem, and his request was from the bottom of his heart.

All this hung in the air as the emperor asked sincerely: "What merit have I earned?"

And to all of this Bodhidharma replied, simply, quietly, "No merit."

This was shocking. After all, Bodhidharma was addressing an emperor with great power. Even though there was a prohibition on capital punishment, he could have ordered Bodhidharma's immediate execution. Not sure how to react to this monk's disconcerting response, the emperor asked, "Who are you? Who are you to dare to respond like this?"

"I do not know," replied Bodhidharma.

Perhaps the death of that other monk long before hung in the back of the emperor's mind, of his heart. I suspect so. But there's something more going on, even for the emperor. And so, stunned, he let the insulting monk leave the imperial presence without punishment.

Later he asked his spiritual advisor about this encounter and was told, "Bodhidharma is none other than the bodhisattva Avalokiteshvara, the manifestation of compassion in this world." Emperor Wu felt waves of shame at missing the opportunity. He decided to send some soldiers to find the monk and return him to the court. But his advisor said, "It's too late. You can send armies, but you will not be able to bring him back."

The moment presented. That moment passed.

For his part, Bodhidharma crossed the river and traveled up-country, settling into a cave not far from the now-renowned Shaolin Temple. He sat there for nine years, facing a cave wall— before a student appeared.

THAT'S THE STORY, powerful and compelling.

The history, as is often the case with such things, is much more murky. In the surviving literature, the name *Bodhidharma* appears here and there. There was once someone called Bodhidharma, possibly a Persian, who marveled at a great city. Someone else named Bodhidharma wrote a treatise on the Great Way. Maybe the same monk, maybe not.

Bodhidharma is a will-o'-the-wisp, appearing in mists, whispering something, but exactly what isn't clear. Not knowing is like that, isn't it?

He is more like a dream or something appearing in the corner of the eye. You can't quite capture the truth of the person, but you can't see him at all straight on.

It is here the mystery of Zen's lineage appears. And it turns on Bodhidharma's words, "I do not know"—on not knowing. Not knowing is forgetting. Not knowing is losing. Not knowing comes closest to a volitional act when it is a letting go. But really, this not knowing is a gift.

In fact, it isn't until some two hundred years after these events play out, sometime in the middle of the eighth century, that we get the broad outlines of this story about that emperor and that monk. The story was first published as an appendix to an edition of the Platform Sutra of the Sixth Ancestor.

And it is the Platform Sutra that gives us the second key story from China's unique take on Buddhism that is Zen. For me, this is perhaps the most important of the stories. It begins with an illiterate peasant and a turning word. We encounter an impoverished woodcutter, his discovery, and what happened because of that finding.

HUINENG was born in the middle of the seventh century, in the southern Guangdong province. His father had been a government official who had been stripped of his rank and exiled there. Very likely he died when Huineng was an infant. The boy had to work as soon as he was able to support himself and his mother. It is said he never learned to read or write.

As a young man, barely beyond childhood, Huineng was delivering firewood when he heard a customer reciting from a popular Buddhist text, the Diamond Sutra. The account doesn't tell us what part of the sutra caught him. Some say it's the line

"Let your mind flow freely without dwelling on anything." However, the most famous line in the Diamond Sutra is the *gatha*, a short verse that concludes the text:

> So you should view this fleeting world—
> A star at dawn, a bubble in a stream,
> A flash of lightning in a summer cloud,
> A flickering lamp, a phantom, and a dream.

The boy exclaimed his wonder at this revelation and asked the man where he had learned this amazing teaching. The man replied that he had heard it from the lips of the great teacher Daman Hongren. In the story of lineage Hongren was the fifth-generation successor to the great master Bodhidharma.

Huineng concluded that he had to study with the master. In one version of the story, he immediately takes off on his quest, leaving us to wonder whether he simply abandoned his mother. In another, more loved version, the customer sympathizes with the boy's burning desire and donates a hundred taels of silver to support Huineng's mother—more than enough to last for the rest of her life.

In this version, only upon having his filial responsibilities fulfilled, Huineng undertakes the journey. It is difficult and dangerous. But finally he arrives at the monastery where he is granted an audience with Master Hongren. The venerable monk looks at the boy who has been ushered into his rooms for the interview and asks, "Why are you here?"

Huineng says simply, "I am here to learn to be a Buddha."

Knowing the boy had come from the south of China, the old man laughs and says, "Nothing of value has ever come from the South." (We can imagine some Americans expressing similar words, and for similarly prejudiced reasons.)

The boy replies, "There is no North nor South in the Buddha Way. Your holiness and I are different, yes. But we are also the same."

The master liked the answer and admitted the boy to the monastery as a lay monk. He was set to work in the kitchen. Lay monks did not meditate, nor did they learn or perform the liturgies. Young Huineng's practice was simply the work he did in the kitchen.

He continued working in the monastery kitchen for the next eight months. If he saw the meditation hall at all it was probably while carrying a bucket of water to scrub floors. He might have sat in the back of the ceremonial hall for liturgy, but only as a member of the congregation. His practices were the arts of the kitchen, cleaning, and prepping food. He wouldn't even have been the cook. At the same time, those turning words that brought Huineng there continued to burrow into his heart, revealing themselves in every dish he washed as he washed it, every pot he scrubbed as he scrubbed it.

Finally there came a moment when the old master decided it was time to name a successor. This was difficult for him because there was no one really ready. Still, he was aging and knew he needed to find someone. So the master announced there would be a contest: anyone within the monastery was welcome to write a word on an interior wall expressing his best insight. Based on those poems, the master would choose his successor.

The person who felt the most pressure to produce that word was the head monk, Shenxiu. He was hesitant. Even though he had attended his master for much of a lifetime—and he had achieved some insight—he knew in his heart of hearts he had not penetrated all the way into the Great Matter itself. Still, he felt the necessity of responsibility and composed a verse, writing it on the wall.

> The body is the Bodhi tree,
> The mind is like a clear mirror.
> At all times we must strive to polish it
> And must not let the dust collect.

When Hongren saw the verse his heart was broken. His senior student had not seen through to the heart of the matter.

Still, the verse had truth about it, and so he said aloud to the gathered assembly, "These are wise words." No one else dared to offer another comment. Most felt the master's successor had been found.

Huineng was ignorant of these goings on, and he later came upon the verse standing alone on the wall. Being illiterate, he had to ask a monk to read it to him. When he heard the words, he said, "No, no. That's not right." And he asked the monk to write his spontaneous response on the wall:

> Bodhi originally has no tree,
> The mirror has no stand.
> Buddha-nature is always clean and pure;
> Where is there room for dust?

The next day Hongren saw these words and immediately exclaimed out loud, "What nonsense!"—and ordered the verse wiped away. But then he quietly inquired into who had written them. That night he sent for Huineng.

The old master questioned the young lay monk closely and heard his account of waking at hearing a passage from the Diamond Sutra. Realizing Huineng had not yet heard the whole text, he then recited it to the young man. Upon hearing the words, "Let your mind flow freely without dwelling on anything," Huineng had his complete awakening into the Great Way.

There's another version of the story, recorded in the koan collections. In the version recorded in Master Keizan's *Record of the Transmission of the Lamp*, the old master entered the shed where the young man slept. As soon as the young man awakened and made his bows, the master immediately asked, "Is the rice white?" Huineng replied, "It is. But it has not been sifted." Hongren took his staff and struck the mortar in the room three times. In response, Huineng picked up the sifting basket and shook it three times.

We don't know which account of the encounter between Hongren and Huineng is more accurate, whether it was the recital of the Diamond Sutra or the mysterious koanic exchange. In any case, the master gave the young lay monk his staff, his bowl, and his robe. And with those acts he declared Huineng his heir—the sixth ancestor in direct succession from Bodhidharma, who was himself the twenty-eighth successor from the Buddha. The old monk also warned him that his life would be in danger if he stayed in the monastery. He said, "Flee to the mountains and hide for the next three years. Then teach."

Huineng immediately left but quickly realized he was being pursued. Eventually one of the monks, a former general named Ming, caught up with him. The young master set the staff, bowl, and robe on the ground explaining, "These are mere symbols. Take them."

Ming reached for the robe and bowl, but he couldn't lift them. Then, sweat pouring off of him, he stepped back and looked at the young lay monk, and said, "I have no need of symbols. Please convey the truth to me."

Huineng replied, "Don't think good. Don't think ill. At this moment, just ask yourself, 'What is my original face?'"

These became Ming's turning words.

He immediately saw into the Great Matter and had his own awakening. Ming then asked, "Now that I have seen my original face, are there any other secret teachings to convey?"

Huineng replied, "What I've conveyed is not a secret. There are no secret teachings."

And with that, Ming declared, "I see now that you are my teacher."

"Well, if you can say that, then we are both heirs to Master Hongren."

The former general returned to the monastery, while Huineng continued on into the mountains and his three-year retreat.

ALL ZEN LINEAGES flow through Huineng, and the Zen Way takes its shape out of Huineng's story. The actual historicity of this encounter is unclear. The story is actually originally written down as part of a polemic on behalf of one Zen school hoping to assert its superiority over another. Just to complicate things, the written version itself has considerable variation from one document to another.

At the same time, the Zen school really is shaped by Hongren, Huineng, their successors, and their teachings. It is a Zen caught up with the creative tension of "gradual awakening" and "sudden awakening"—a tension that would recur over and over again within the Zen schools.

There are two things going on within the dynamic of the emerging Zen schools: cultivation and awakening. How they relate remains complex, mysterious, and never fully catchable within one side or the other.

# 3

# The Cradle of Zen

As Buddhism began to spread through China, it appears that many in the early generations of practitioners were as well versed in the Confucian and Daoist classics as they were in the Buddhist texts. From the beginning, we see the many elements of a perhaps unavoidable synthesis.

One element of this synthesis was the early adoption of traditional Chinese terms to replace traditional Buddhist words. Quickly, these new words began to subtly change meanings. No word is more representative of this dynamic encounter than the Buddhist adoption of the Chinese word *Dao*.

In Buddhist usage *Dao* (or *Tao* in earlier transliterations) sometimes refers to a "way," a literal road or path. However, it is also meant to be the *Buddhist Way* specifically. The Buddhists who adopted the term incorporated the several meanings of the Sanskrit word *Dharma* into *Dao*. No doubt done innocently in an attempt to make the new teaching comprehensible, this shift came to have enormous consequences.

The independent scholar and Rinzai Zen priest Ruth Fuller Sasaki (possibly the first Western Rinzai Zen priest) discusses this in her magisterial *Zen Dust*, written with Isshu Miura. Dao's new "meaning is more closely akin to that in Daoism; it is the Absolute, the Ultimate Principle, Truth, Reason, the indescribable source of all existence and all manifested phenomena."

Here something new is birthing. Here we find a Buddhism that both is and is not the Buddhism of India. What we have is an encounter that is complex and rich. In dealing with the realities of Chinese culture and religion, Buddhism takes on new colors, and new areas of emphasis.

One example is the concept of lineage: the idea that the teachings are handed down in unbroken line from one person to one person. Who your parents are is not of any particular importance to Indians—however, it is a very Chinese concern. As Zen emerges as a distinctive school, it reports a lineage passing from the Buddha to Mahakashyapa and on through twenty-seven generations to Bodhidharma.

And it is Bodhidharma who goes to China and becomes the first of the Chinese generations transmitting Zen. The lineage leads to the sixth successor, Huineng, and from him to all the existing Zen lines.

One convention among contemporary scholars is to debunk lineage in its entirety. However, that actually isn't all that helpful. While the new form of Chinese Buddhism is quite different from its origins in important ways, it is also firmly rooted in the Indian Buddhist teachings. There definitely is a strong family resemblance. And so, while the Indian lineage is perhaps not quite so clear in its genealogy as Chinese Buddhists made it out to be, there are Indian ancestors.

It is also worthwhile to consider other innovations of this new tradition rising in China. These earliest meditators for the most part started with reading. Which is a delicious irony for a tradition that became famous for standing "outside" the necessity of texts. Inspired by their reading they began to seek out meditation masters, both for instruction and for verification.

It's entirely possible that these early meditation masters were themselves the product of reading, with relatively little training in practice. Still, through a process of trial and error, consulting both Buddhist and non-Buddhist meditators, some of these practitioners made profound discoveries about who they were and what the world was.

Some of these teachers began to attract communities of students. Mostly monks and nuns, these new students spent years with their teachers before they grew mature enough in their practice to return to their own hermitages or monasteries—or their government offices. And some of them went on to teach students of their own.

Over the next two hundred years, communities grew up around differing styles focused on "contemplation of the mind." Here Zen's technologies of the spirit begin to appear, as do Zen lineages in a historical sense.

However, it isn't until the seventh century and the fifth patriarch, Daman Hongren, that we begin to see lineage as a historic fact. All existing Zen lineages today derive through Hongren and his successor Huineng. Zen schools may differ, but all share the origin story of Hongren's robe and bowl. And what was a story became a historical fact.

So lineages are neither some quasi-magical manifestations of "mind-to-mind transmission" nor are they wholly unrelated to our understanding of a deeper reality than we usually perceive. The Zen project is about this world and our lives, memories, and dreams, as well as our simple comings and goings. The story of lineage is absolutely important. There is something that emerges out of those shades of myth into history, an authentic spiritual path with disciplines and trained spiritual directors.

# 4

# Zen Takes Shape

In TIME, the practices that are unique to Zen take their mature form. *Silent illumination* and *shikantaza* (just sitting) are related to the older Buddhist practices of *shamatha* and *vipassana*—but also owe much to indigenous Chinese, mostly Daoist, meditation disciplines.

As to the other unique-to-Zen practice—koan introspection—Ruth Fuller Sasaki suggests that it emerges on the cusp of the ninth and tenth centuries, in the thirteenth generation from Huineng. Master Nanyuan Huiyong appears to be the first teacher to embrace "the use of the words of earlier masters in a fixed and systematized form to instruct or test a student."

What emerged as Zen was a new way of approaching the great matters of life and death, our broken hearts, and our healing. Wendy Egyoku Nakao, Zen priest and abbot of the Zen Center of Los Angeles, frames the endeavor this way: "Zen Buddhism speaks to liberation, to fully realizing and freely living this journey wherever we are, however we are, in whatever circumstances we find ourselves, including relationships, family life, and work."

In his study *Seeing Through Zen*, John McRae describes the development of this teaching style writ large:

> Here the locus of religious practice was firmly removed from individual effort in the meditation hall and replaced by a demanding genre of interrogation that sought to destabilize all habitual, logical patterns. Spontaneity was the rule, iconoclastic behavior the norm.

McRae then continues, "Or so it seems."

A blending of respect for this view and a healthy dollop of suspicion is probably in order.

I find it interesting to note how long it is before we begin to see evidence of a systematic approach in the literature. The eighth-century master Shitou Xiqian's masterworks, the "Sandokai" and the "Song of the Grass-Roof Hermitage," are evocative of the heart of the practices of meditation. However, it isn't until the first half of the twelfth century that Hongzhi Zhengjue writes of silent illumination and Dahui Zonggao writes of koan introspection. These are among the first clear expositions of how the practices were taught.

In the thirteenth century, there will be further development with Dogen's masterful treatise on practice. Still later, the koan curriculum is revitalized and flourishes in Hakuin's school. But we get ahead of the story.

Nonetheless, one can argue that the practices of silent illumination and koan introspection, as they're taught today, began to coalesce in this earlier era.

# 5

# Zen's Way of Awakening

THE PROJECT OF ZEN is about waking up.

Truly, in some sense, all of religion is about awakening, its realization, and the establishment of paths to it. Spiritual awakening is our common human inheritance. It is not exclusive to Zen or Buddhism or any religion.

For me the Heart Sutra is one of the gifts of Zen's way of awakening. Anyone who visits any Zen center in North America has heard it. The Heart Sutra is very short, and its message is so telegraphic that the subtlety and depth of its teaching can easily be missed. Because it ends with a mantra, a sacred phrase, some believe that merely chanting it has some magical efficacy. And maybe it does. But the magic happens by inviting the heart of it to enter our hearts.

Here's my paraphrase of it.

When the Heart of Compassion walked through the

gate of wisdom, she looked into the body of the world and of each of us, seeing that each of us and the world itself is boundless. And with this all suffering vanished.

Dear ones, all things are boundless; the boundless is nothing other than all things. Everything in itself is boundless; boundlessness is all things. This is true of our bodies, feelings, experiences, perceptions, and consciousness itself.

Dear ones, the stuff of the universe is boundless. It is not born; it does not die. It is not impure, nor is it pure. It neither increases nor diminishes. And so within boundlessness there are no sense organs, no objects to sense, and no field of experience; no ignorance and thus no ending of ignorance; no old age and death and thus no ending of old age and death. There is no suffering, no causes of suffering; and thus no path to follow and no wisdom to attain.

Understanding this boundlessness, the pure-hearted one is free. Without entanglements the true person of the Way is not afraid.

This is the pure and unexcelled Way. All the sages of past, present, and future attain to this truth and find freedom. And so the truth of it becomes the great mantra,

supreme and unexcelled; it removes all suffering.
Gone, gone, gone beyond. Completely gone beyond.
Blessings and blessings!

It is part of a collection of texts called the Prajnaparamitas, or Perfection of Wisdom texts. They were written in Sanskrit over many years, starting roughly in the first century before our Common Era. The Heart Sutra stands out as the epitome or summary of the whole body of the Prajnaparamita cycle, reducing a very large library of teachings to fourteen stanzas of thirty-two syllables each—or 260 Chinese characters.

Its exact date of composition is hotly debated, with some scholars even suggesting it was originally composed in Chinese and translated back into Sanskrit. The earliest dates attributed for its composition lie between the first and second centuries of our Common Era, the latest somewhere in the eighth century.

To understand what it points to we need to understand two terms. The first, *skandha* (literally "heap," or maybe "stuff"), is meant to stand for the parts of which we are all composed. The traditional list is form or matter, sensations or feeling, perception, mental formations or impulses, and consciousness or discernment. It's an attempt to describe how we're put together, what the critical bits are, what form is.

The second is emptiness. In Sanskrit the term is *shunyata*, translated most commonly as "emptiness," but also as "void," "open," "spacious." I personally find the term *boundless* a bit less misleading. At the heart of the Heart is a radical assertion about reality. In the most common translations it states, "form is emptiness, emptiness is form."

The modern Korean Zen missionary master Seung Sahn tries to explain what it means by way of an example:

Here is a wooden chair. It is brown. It is solid and heavy. It looks like it could last a long time. You sit in the chair, and it holds up your weight. You can place things on it. But then you light the chair on fire and leave. When you come back later, the chair is no longer there! This thing that seemed so solid and strong and real is now just a pile of cinder and ash, which the wind blows around.

This example shows how the chair is empty: it is not a permanent, abiding thing. It is always changing. It has no independent existence. Over a long or short time, the chair will eventually change and become something other than what it appears. So this brown chair is complete emptiness. But though it always has the quality of emptiness, this emptiness is form: you can sit in the chair, and it will still hold you up.

We are real, you and I. Pinch me, and I guarantee it hurts. And at the same time we exist only within causal relationships. The me that is real is also very temporary. I'm the product, as you are, of many different situations coming together in a glorious moment. I exist as a moment, which in a heartbeat will shift. And I, the part that thinks "I," will be gone.

But to think this merely means we live for a brief period of time and then are food for worms is vastly too reductive; it is a parody of a vastly more wonderful truth. So let's put aside the brown chair, which the master means to use only as an analogy for something, something very important for all of us. This is about a lot more than brown chairs. It is about you, and it is about me, and what is true about us.

The first and critical point here is that no part of us has an existence outside of the phenomenal world. There is no special bit, no "I," no soul that is untouched by the vagaries of life or that escapes death. We are invited to let go of our concept that we are somehow special and not of this world. We are invited into a place of radical interdependence.

While we are all inherently temporary, there's a deeper point, that this temporariness also runs right through what we are at this moment. The Western-born Zen master Bernie Glassman says, "Emptiness is just everything, just as it is right now." John Crook, another Western Zen master, tells us that when we catch this, our "notion of everything as empty now expands and expands until everything you can think of, the vast cosmos itself, is seen as Vast Emptiness. Vastness unlimited, unbounded spaciousness, timeless presence."

Here is the great emptiness, identical with each and every thing rising and falling within the web of relationships that is our life. It can be approached philosophically, but it is in fact a pointer toward our own deepest encounter. Nothing less.

To understand the Heart Sutra and with it Zen's awakening, it is also important to understand the *two truths* and *original awakening*. These are terms that both accurately point—and can terribly mislead.

The *two truths* is the teaching that we are real, existing in this causal world, rising and falling as conditions arise and change. And at the same time, each of these conditions and we ourselves have no abiding substance. While this is implicit in earlier Buddhist teachings, we find they become explicit through a consideration of two traditional Mahayana doctrines. First, *tathagatagarbha*, the doctrine of our universal potential, the assurance we all will achieve buddhahood. And then there's *buddhadatu*, the doctrine of buddha nature. In Zen these terms are collapsed together to describe the exact identity of the causal world and awakening.

The most dangerous thing about the two truths is that it can encourage a dualistic world-view, a mind-spirit split from the body-material world. We find this linguistic difficulty leading people down unhappy paths all the time. Similar objections have been raised in regard to original awakening. The example I am constantly reminded of is that when a company's reckless dumping of chemicals into a harbor ended up poisoning the residents, a part of their defense was that they were all part of the natural world and these actions and consequences were simply inevitable. The court also found their conviction inevitable. So that sophistry can be reinforced by an egocentric embrace of the two truths.

But that's missing the point. What we have with the two truths, and with buddha nature, is a pointing to the nature of reality. I would go further and say a direct pointing. This insight becomes a pointing to our heart's healing.

And so, as the Zen teacher Dosho Port tells us, when the sutra declares, "no eyes,"

That does not mean that we don't have eyes, just as "no attainment" doesn't mean that devotedly practicing the buddhadharma will result in no (in the usual sense of the word) attainment. "No" just means that from the yes to attainment and beyond there is nothing but vastness, no holy—just this vividly hopping along life and death.

"Form is emptiness, emptiness is form." I find this particular passage a declaration of who and what we are, and a pointer for those of us who would find the great peace in the midst of this roiling sea.

This is why the Zen teacher Rachel Mansfield-Howlett tells us, "I discovered an even broader truth: that my body is the same as the redwood, the mountains and rivers, oceans and kelp forests, and the great earth itself."

This path is not about being special. It is about something else entirely. It is a path of engagement, and it is a path of letting go. I was talking with my friend and teaching colleague Josh Bartok about the terms *entrusting* and *true entrusting*. He likes them and in his teaching uses them a lot. However, they are mostly used in the Shin Buddhist tradition, and not so much by Zen people.

I asked him if there was an obvious Zen usage of that "entrusting"? He replied that we can find it right there in the title of the *Xinxinming*, one of the central texts of the Zen Way, written by the second Chinese ancestor of Zen, Sengcan. The Chinese *Xinxin* ( Jap: *shinjin*; 信心) can be translated as "faith mind" or, equally accurately, as "the entrusting heart" or "true entrusting."

And this is indeed what we're about on this path. This path of ours is one of mind and it is one of heart—and absolutely it is all about entrusting ourselves to and within unfolding reality. There is a quality of our taking our fate in our hands, but also there is a quality of surrender into mysterious reality. Awakening has to do with all this.

However, even if we can't quite express the deepest experience of our hearts with precision, we can bring images and allusions to help us. What follows is my small attempt at putting words, images, and allusions to that something which can't be captured by descriptive language alone. This book is an invitation into the poetry of our lives.

So remember, the Heart Sutra, like our lives, is poetry. And the poetry of Zen points to the heart's awakening, that true entrusting into the mysterious reality that is this world. The disciplines, the practices all have this one point—the healing of a broken world, and with that the healing of our own broken hearts.

This is Zen's awakening.

PART TWO

# The Practices of Zen

# 6

# The Body of Zen

We start with the body.

In 1982 Robert Aitken wrote *Taking the Path of Zen*. For many years it was the definitive introduction to Zen practice in the English language, and it remains a classic. Aitken Roshi tells us that "posture is the form of Zen." The practice is all about embodiment, so attending to how we use and place our bodies is very much at the heart of the practice. And moreover, as Master Dogen tells us, "The entire universe is the true human body. The entire universe is the Dharma body of the self."

That said, let's look at part of this true human body in meditation. The Buddha said there were four postures for meditation: sitting, standing, lying down, and walking. However, for many reasons sitting has become the baseline posture of the discipline. In the Zen schools derived from Japan we use two pillows to assist in sitting.

The first is the *zafu*, a small round pillow, traditionally stuffed with kapok, the fiber of the *Ceiba pentandra* tree. Zafus stuffed with buckwheat hulls have become steadily more popular in the West, and today they are my preference. The traditional size is about fourteen inches in diameter and eight inches high. Smaller and larger pillows are not uncommon. I prefer a slightly larger zafu.

The meditator sits to the front half of the pillow, allowing the knees to fall to the ground—or better, letting them rest on the second cushion, a *zabuton*. The zabuton is a rectangular cushion of cotton batting, traditionally about thirty inches by twenty-eight inches, and an inch or two thick. It has an outer casing of some sturdy material and provides support for the knees and the ankles.

Traditionally, we are encouraged to sit in either the full-lotus or the half-lotus positions. Some will go so far as to say anything else is not zazen. Resting one foot on the opposite calf rather than on the thigh is called the quarter-lotus or in some circles the half-ass lotus. If the foot is placed directly on the ground rather than resting on the thigh or calf, it is called Burmese. All of these positions are common in Zen groups.

A major variation from this cross-legged sitting is *seiza*. *Seiza* means "proper sitting" in Japanese. I've heard it colloquially translated as "sitting as human beings sit," an interesting comment on cultural relativism. *Seiza* is kneeling while resting your buttocks on your heels. The pressure on the knees and top of one's feet can be relieved by sitting on a zafu that has been placed sideways between the legs.

In the West this is often assisted with a seiza bench. The bench is a plank serving as the seat, sometimes padded, about twenty inches long and seven or so inches deep. It rests on braces about seven inches high and cut at a slight angle to assist in the drop of the knees. The meditator uses this with a traditional zabuton supporting the knees and top of the feet.

One may also simply sit in a chair. Ideally, the height from the seat to the floor allows the meditator to sit toward the front of the chair, allowing the knees to drop several inches. The legs spread at a comfortable angle, with the feet resting flat on the floor. This supports the torso in a manner similar to the variations on the lotus or seiza positions.

Each of these positions support the torso in its upright posture. Sitting up "straight" produces the slight *S* curve that occurs naturally as you push the small of the back slightly forward and pull the shoulders slightly back. This opens the chest cavity, allowing air to flow easily through the lungs.

One teacher, when asked what is important in zazen, simply replied, "Breathing and posture." After a moment he corrected himself and said, "Posture." The upright spine is the single most important part of the traditional Zen meditation posture.

The chin is tucked slightly in. Hands can rest in the lap in the cosmic mudra, where one hand rests on the other, both palms up. The thumb-tips touch, forming a circle. This is the style used in nearly all Soto-based communities. Another style, where one thumb is grasped by the opposite hand, is the style preferred in many Rinzai communities.

In Zen, nearly uniquely among meditation disciplines, the eyes are kept open. Usually the eyes are opened up from just a fraction to about a half an inch. The gaze falls forward, but without focusing on anything in particular. It avoids obsessing on a particular spot, but it doesn't go completely unfocused, either. Sometimes this is called a "gentle gaze."

There is also a form of walking meditation in Zen called *kinhin*. In kinhin the hands are held at the lower abdomen, at the solar plexus, called the *hara* or *tanden*. Kinhin is most commonly done between periods of seated meditation. It is usually done in a line with other meditators, following the leader who sets the pace. The pace is varied from group to group, some introducing two periods, one slower, the other faster. In traditional Soto communities the pace can be very slow, while in some Rinzai ones kinhin can even be brisk.

In most Soto schools meditators sit facing a wall or screen. In most Rinzai schools meditators sit facing into the community. Both choices have advantages and disadvantages. The invitation for the individual meditator is to lean into the community's discipline and to practice with everyone else.

It can be a very powerful experience.

# 7

# The Art of Breathing

THE PRACTICE OF ZEN is presence. So, as Zen teacher Josh Bartok points out, "zazen is done sitting *in presence to* breath, sitting *in presence to* mind, sitting *in presence to* body. It is body, breath, and mind harmoniously 'zazening.'" In Zen, this fundamental practice of presence, our "zazening" principally takes the form of *just sitting*.

However, as it turns out, that just sitting is, in some sense, a very hard thing to do. Fortunately, we also have other practices, breath-counting or breath-following—mindfulness of the breath. The Buddha himself taught mindfulness of breath, a practice he used when he was a student on the Way himself. It is an ancient practice.

Once I had a light brush with pneumonia. In the midst of it, I had a powerful dream. I was suffocating—and I wasn't. I could feel the air shutting off. At the same time, I was aware I was in fact breathing. I'd fallen into some liminal space between sleep and waking, where the dream was driven by the reality of my pneumonia. But another part, a "waking" part, knew that I really was breathing, if not optimally. The experience could make anyone appreciate the ability to take a deep breath, even if, as at that moment, it hurts a bit.

Now my brush with pneumonia was a brush. Hearing and reading stories of how serious it can be, I was grateful that it wasn't worse. But I also knew pneumonia needs to be treated with respect. I had to cancel some very important meetings and a conference, where I was scheduled to be a presenter. Breath is, after all, that important.

Because we have to breathe anyway, we realize why breath-counting is a perfect way to practice Zen meditation. Our breathing will go on whether we are noticing or not. When we start counting our breaths we see how easy it is to lose our concentration. We try to follow our breathing, and when we fail we can still return to it, at least until we stop breathing forever. For the most part, in Zen practice, mindfulness of breath is a preliminary step. But in some ways it is the whole practice.

The nature of the traditional Zen posture inclines us to dia-phragmatic breathing, filling our lungs from the bottom. It is common to recommend that the breathing be slow, deliberate, and deep. This isn't critical in Zen practice. Although for some among us it can be important. Sometimes slightly controlling the exhalation so that it is long, perhaps adding in a gentle push at the end of that exhalation, can be helpful.

In the Kwan Um School of Zen, meditators may bring a mantra into the breath practice. Inhale to a count of three, repeating the phrase "clear mind" on each of the counts. Then exhale to a count of seven repeating the single phrase "only don't know" throughout the count.

The lay Rinzai teacher Katsuki Sekida recommended what he called *bamboo* or *segmented breathing*. First, take a deep breath. Then exhale until about a quarter of the air is gone from your lungs. Pause. Continue to exhale until about half the air is gone. Pause again. Exhale completely, pushing all the air out. Then inhale, pausing as the lungs are about half full. Then complete the inhalation.

Then take three normal breaths, pausing in each breath cycle at the halfway point and at the turning from inhalation to exhalation. Repeat—one deep breath with the pauses as described, and three normal breaths with those pauses. Mr. Sekida recommended joining this breathing practice to the Mu koan. We will return to this when we come to koan introspection.

In my opinion, Rinzai master Shodo Harada gives the most helpful breathing instruction one can find in the Zen context. He starts by calling us to center our breathing in the solar plexus. Breathe in through the nostrils, then exhale using the mouth, at least for a couple of breaths, and add that little push at the end, completely emptying the lungs. Then move into a more natural breathing pattern in and out through the nostrils.

The respiration should be neither overly forceful nor overly gentle—it should feel full and expansive, as though it extends infinitely and without constraint. The breath should feel as though it comes not from the chest but directly from the lower abdomen, as though there were an open pipe directly connecting the tanden and the mouth.

Before long, tensions release as the consciousness settles naturally into the solar plexus. Continue to add that push at the end of the exhalation. The Zen priest and teacher Mitra Bishop calls this "the extended out-breath." Shodo Harada Roshi actually says that this extended out-breath *is* Zen meditation.

I hope you've noticed that, a few pages back, we quoted several Zen teachers who say that upright posture is Zen meditation. I believe there is much to be found in the apparent contradiction. Is sitting upright the point of Zen practice, or is it the extended out-breath? Neither? Both? Again, if we surrender any idea of a strict instrumentality, we are given that wonderful invitation.

With or without the extended out-breath, the posture itself leads the practitioner into abdominal or diaphragmatic breathing. The body will flood with the extra oxygenation, and with that a calming of the mind naturally follows. As you continue you will probably feel the thoughts and concerns of the day leaving along with the exhalation. It is common to fairly quickly find a spacious place. Harada Roshi describes what this can look like:

When you have settled into this abdominal breathing, with the shoulders and chest free of tension, the entire upper body relaxed, and your strength seated in the *tanden*, then a shift takes place—from abdominal breathing to tanden breathing. In the former, the abdominal muscles play the major role in the drawing in and letting out of the breath, expanding and contracting to enable long, relaxed, free respiration. This quickly brings about a settling of *ki* (chi, energy) in the tanden, which in turn gives rise to a sense of strength and stability in the area between the lower back and the lower abdomen, drawing the consciousness there and filling it with relaxed energy. In this state, the abdomen remains rounded and nearly motionless even as the breath moves freely in and out, as though (in the words of Hakuin) there were a fully inflated ball inside. Were the belly to be poked from the outside, it would feel taut and firm but not rigid.

As we see there are a surprising number of ways to bring breath into our practice. In my Zen community we do one of the simplest forms, and I recommend it for most of us. We counsel a simple and bare attention to the movement of the breath. Just notice. It's surprising how often we don't; sometimes we even can't.

So we recommend breath-counting. Counting one for the first inhalation, two for the second. Count up to ten. And then start over. If you don't make it to ten, just notice that, and start over. When we notice we've lost count there can be a temptation to ascribe responsibility or blame. Some people blame themselves. There is a similar temptation to blame others, your neighbor's grumbling stomach, or noise outside the room. Of course, what was a distraction has now become a metadistraction. Let go of the blame, and return to one. Just return to one.

Sometimes people find it difficult to recall the ordering of the numbers. There's a simple strategy of letting the count fill the inhalation or exhalation. So, *ooooonnnne* for whatever the natural length of the breath is. Again, without controlling it, just witnessing it. *Twwwwoooo* on the exhalation. And so on . . .

We don't normally recommend any attempt at controlling the breath, not even that little extra push at the end of the exhalation. That said, some experimentation can be wise.

And whether you settle upon letting the breath flow naturally, adding that extended out-breath, or one of the other variations practiced within Zen, the real point is to let the breathing breathe.

Of course thoughts will arise. Shunryu Suzuki Roshi notes how our thoughts come and go. That's fine, he tells us, and adds, "Just don't invite them for tea." Notice, and let go. Notice, and return to the practice.

As you become more experienced with the practice, you might choose to count only the exhalations. I recommend continuing this practice until it becomes relatively easy to maintain your concentration. Whether it's for a few weeks, a few months, a year, or two. It doesn't really matter. Just keep on doing it.

The great eighteenth-century master Hakuin Ekaku recommended trying to count those inhalations and exhalations (or just the exhalations) to ten. But then he adds a suggestion. If you want to push the concentration part of the practice, try counting to a hundred. If that's not hard enough, try going to a thousand. Each attempt can bring things to us. But really, going to ten is sufficient.

If counting to ten proves too difficult, you might experiment with a shorter count. Perhaps it's eight. Maybe it's three. Find the number you get to regularly and make the "goal" one breath more. So if you get to three with some consistency, make the practice counting to four. No blame here; just pay attention to what's happening.

Let the breathing flow in and out. And then, whether we're counting or not, whether we just breathe naturally or we add in that small extra push at the end of the exhalation, we begin to notice things. We see the contours of our thoughts. This might be revelatory at first. And then the repetition of our thoughts might actually become boring after a while. Turns out, we human beings kind of like to wallow in the same mess for long periods of time. We're angry. We want. We tell ourselves stories along well-worn trails.

But notice, and breathe, and return to one, over and over. Then maybe something breaks out of this. We notice we're really noticing. We notice the connections. We notice the words we attach to the experience are just words that are attached to the experience. This noticing is the same as the Buddha's bare attention. Some say this noticing is Zen meditation.

Just return. Bring a bare attention to it all. And all along keep on breathing, like Old Man River, just rolling along, in and out, in and out. Notice. Worlds emerge, flower, and fall away. Empires are created. Love stories unfold. Fights break out. The whole shebang plays out as we breathe, in and out, in and out. Just notice.

Expanding upon this, Josh Bartok explains:

Many people tend to locate the seat of our consciousness in the center of our head, behind the eyes, and we breathe from there—or we imagine we are somehow monitoring our breath from there. But in this practice of zazen we breathe from the hara, which is around three fingers below the navel, near the diaphragm, holding our center of attention there.

It can be helpful to imagine taking hold of that single point of awareness that seems to be in the center of the head behind the eyes and imaginally pulling it down to the hara, and then breathing from there, meeting the breath from the hara rather than head. When the mind moves back into thought, the feeling of center-of-self may move right back up to head—and when we notice that this has happened, we imaginally take hold of it and imaginally bring it back down, continuing to breathe from the hara.

Another image that may help with this is a plunger gently descending on our head, pushing gently down. Breathing out, the plunger doesn't go up. Breathing in, coming down; breathing out, not going up. Or we can feel the pull of gravity downward from the hara, the physical center of our bodily mass, and breathe from there.

But however we practice, it's important to breathe with the entirety of body-breath-mind-and-universe—not just mind, not just body, not just breath. Body-breath-mind-and-universe breathes body-breath-mind-and-universe.

Over time, and particularly sitting for longer periods, this practice does take one into *samadhi* states, those places of deep calm and presence. The invitation is to not chase after states, however beautiful. As one Zen wag observed, "states are just states." They arise and fall apart like everything else. The secret is just sitting and breathing and noticing. Nothing more is needed.

This is Zen meditation.

# 8

# Samadhi

CASE 67 of the anthology *Book of Serenity*, contains this koan, which is simply a line from the Huayan Sutra: "Now when I look at all beings everywhere, I see that each of them possesses the wisdom and virtue of the Tathagata, but because of their attachment and delusion, they cannot bear witness to it."

I suggest this sentence contains the essentials of Zen meditation, including the details of how and to what purpose we take on this practice. Koans make assertions from the standpoint of wisdom and invite responses. This case simply lays it all out for us and invites us into an intimate conversation, a dance with reality. It also shows where koan and silent illumination become a single practice.

Hongzhi Zhengjue lived from the end of the eleventh century through the middle of the twelfth century. He compiled the *Book of Serenity* (also translated as the *Book of Equanimity*), for which all Zen students are eternally indebted to him.

This book features prominently in the Harada-Yasutani Soto-reformed koan curriculum that I practice within.

Hongzhi has a place in Zen folklore, frequently paired with Dahui Zonggao in the great early-twelfth-century Chinese debate team. They dug deeply into the relative merits of just sitting / silent illumination and koan introspection practice. Much of what they say probes the shadows of the two disciplines—which, like so many human endeavors, are rife with possibility and deeply shadowed, all at the same time.

While often depicted as opponents, Dahui and Hongzhi were in fact close friends. Each mastered his own preferred discipline, criticizing the other only in its extreme and exclusionary forms. So the master of just sitting was deeply intimate with the koan way, while the master of the koan never abandoned the cushion in his practice. They are perfect exemplars for us as we follow the path of awakening.

Their warnings are important. The criticism of a one-sided devotion to koan introspection is that it can become arid, intellectual, and disconnected from reality. And a one-sided attachment to a just-sitting practice can slip into torpidity, into a mere quietism. These are accurately perceived; these are problems that have arisen over and over throughout Zen's history. And yet, taken carefully, engaged with heart and body and open eyes, these two are among the most important disciplines of the heart. They are, in my estimation, the culmination of our human technologies of the spirit.

As Hongzhi presented the practice of just sitting, we can see its roots in both vipassana and shamatha. Hongzhi warns, "if illumination neglects serenity then aggressiveness appears." However, "if serenity neglects illumination, murkiness leads to wasted dharma." Commenting on this, Zen priest and scholar Taigen Leighton writes, "Hongzhi's meditation values the balancing of both stopping or settling the mind, and its active illuminating function."

SAMADHI is a term of art used with somewhat different meanings in all the religions that birthed in India. Samadhi is the deep place of Zen, where the breath and mind both slow, and sometimes rising thoughts are barely noticeable. For many Soto teachers this is the *summum bonum* of the Way. And many Rinzai teachers consider samadhi states the seedbed for awakening.

The word has multiple shades of meaning. With Bodhidharma and Huineng it is often a synonym for awakening. And that perspective remains the heart perspective of samadhi. But it is also identified with the states of deep quiet, which touch but are not necessarily the same as awakening. Instead it's a liminal spot, touching awakening, touching being quiet. These deep quiet places are powerful.

I've seen people take to the cushion as an escape from life. The samadhi state is very seductive. When asked why Zen people get so attached to samadhi states, Harada Roshi replied, "Because it feels so good." Dahui warned how such a one-sided romancing of silent illumination is teaching "people to stop and rest and play dead." So we need to be careful.

At the same time, without Zen meditation we're lost. Without the practice of sitting down and paying attention, we find how easy it is to just play games with enlightenment. We take our insight and its expression is limited to a beautiful line of poetry or a nice quip—but it isn't lived into, it doesn't become the reality our lives.

So what is the Middle Way of the Zen disciplines, the authentic heart of them all? I suggest Zen meditation is about the whole of our lives. It is about life and death and everything in between. It is about healing the great hurt that lives near most everyone's heart. We sit not just for ourselves; we sit for the whole world. And this requires diligence.

Zen teacher Doug Philips writes about this:

I was struck by how easily we are pulled from the immediacy of this life in this moment by thoughts of a future that none of us can predict; how easily we abandon our practice of being fully here now for a misery-producing fantasy. It clearly takes great courage and intention to fully embody our actual life when the ground we thought was solid begins to shake, rattle, and roll. And yet this is what we are called to as a life of practice and where the Buddha pointed as the only time and place we will ever have the opportunity to be awake and free.

# 9

# Bearing Witness to the Great Matter

IN the "Song of the Grass-Roof Hermitage" Shitou calls us to "turn around the light to shine within and then just return." Hongzhi says, "turn within and drop off everything completely, and realization will occur." Dogen tells us to "cease practice based on intellectual understanding, pursuing words and following after speech, and learn the backward step that turns your light inwardly to illuminate yourself. Body and mind of themselves will drop away and your original face will be manifest."

Just turn the eye inward, look and notice. The whole thing will reveal itself as it has over many years. For instance, this becomes the stuff of Dogen's awakening. When his master Rujing found the young monk sleeping, he says, "To study the Way is to cast off body/mind. Why are you engaged in single-minded sleeping instead of single-minded sitting?" With these words, Dogen saw into the fundamental matter.

A koan (as we will soon see) is a matter to be made clear. It is a presentation of wisdom and an invitation into presence. Rujing offered the koan of Zen meditation. And, like that box and its lid, Dogen responded. Just sitting becomes the Buddha sitting.

Bearing witness, bare attention. Don't cling to this or that. Just notice. Directly to the point of the case, early in his training, while at Shangshan Temple, Hongzhi heard a monk reciting from the Huayan Sutra: "The eyes that our parents give us can behold three thousand worlds." Hearing this he had his first awakening. Our eyes are the Buddha's eyes—or can be, when we open them.

Yaoshan Weiyan was asked what he thought while sitting. Yaoshan famously replied that he thought of "not-thinking." The questioner pushed and asked how to do that, to which he responded, "Beyond thinking." Master Dogen, perhaps the foremost commentator on the discipline of just sitting, repeated this exchange on a number of occasions.

So what is beyond thinking? It is not as esoteric as it might at first sound. It certainly isn't becoming a bump on a log, and it isn't killing all thoughts. Even in the deepest samadhi states, thoughts are not completely stilled. The truth is, our brains excrete thoughts in much the same way our intestines secrete waste. Thoughts end only with the final disruption of the body.

What we're being invited to is something else. It is taking the whole, being present to it all, without judgment. It is being fully present to this ordinary body that you were given by your parents. And here's the secret teaching: your body has within it a full and complete capacity to know the Buddha's wisdom and virtue. Not someone else's body, but yours. And it isn't found some other place. Rather, it is found here. Just here. Always, just here.

The experience can be astonishing. In *The Hidden Lamp*, a wonderful collection of koans and Buddhist stories, Zen teacher and coabbot of Great Vow Zen Monastery Jan Chozen Bays tells us:

> Zazen allows us to zoom in like a microscope, past skin and hair, sinking into the commonality of bone and flesh, of carbon and hydrogen, all the way down to gluons and quarks dancing in empty space—a field of potential energy filled with forms flashing in and out of existence.

Now there are traps along this Way—a lot of them. Even *kensho* itself (an experience of awakening, about which more later) can be kind of trap. Anything with power is dangerous, of course. And ego is always finding ways to be confirmed. Ironically, this is true even of a practice that deconstructs most of the illusions surrounding our sense of self.

For instance, if I am the Buddha, well, then following my whims and desires, shouldn't that be the Buddha's whims and desires? And in one sense, sure, that's true. But if we take it as an invitation into excesses of various sorts, nothing but sadness follows. Examples of this are as recent as the history of Zen in North America and the harm caused by teachers not held accountable to ethical standards.

The famous debate between Hongshi and Dahui recapitulates the tensions that run through the Zen schools, highlighting emphasis and excess. They represent the two major surviving houses or schools of Zen: Caodong (Soto in Japanese) and Linji (Rinzai in Japanese). While it is overly simplistic, the ways emphasized by Hongshi are associated mostly with the Soto lineages, and the ways emphasized by Dahui are associated mostly with the Rinzai lineages.

The liveliness of *shikantaza* as Hongzhi presents it can become lost with too hard an emphasis on not choosing. Not choosing becoming a central theme of our insight, an openness that excludes nothing. But this has shadows. With too hard an emphasis it falls into a cult of serenity, where zazen becomes a meaningless ritual imitating a long-dead Buddha. This has its rewards, of course. There are always those deep bliss states. They come even if one clings to not choosing, as if it were a life raft in the midst of the raging sea.

Nevertheless, it is missing what the master was calling us to. Zen and Zen's meditation is about something more than a deep sense of contentment. Shikantaza needs to be engaged as something alive and, of course, dangerous. If we take both serenity and illumination as a seamless whole, it opens us to what the Japanese Soto master Hashimoto Eko meant when he said, "Sit down and become Buddha." Here the koan that is Zen meditation is revealed as an assertion and an invitation.

Dogen beautifully presents what this looks like in his essay "Bendowa":

The zazen of even one person at one moment imperceptibly accords with all things and fully accords with all things and fully resonates through all time. Thus in the past, future, and present of the limitless universe this zazen carries on the buddha's teaching endlessly. Each moment of zazen is equally wholeness of practice, equally wholeness of realization.

Zen teacher Josh Bartok introduces a very helpful image for this practice. He calls it "freefall":

In the freefall of shikantaza, we may try to grab on to some form of certainty or some technique to stop our fall, like Wile E. Coyote grabbing on to a branch as he falls off a cliff—and then that branch breaks. In shikantaza we simply see this impulse to grab, without enacting the story of grabbing, or buying into the story of needing to stop our fall, of needing to apply an antidote to some experience. Practicing in freefall in this Way is practicing being comfortable with not knowing, comfortable with uncertainty, comfortable with discomfort, comfortable with doubt and even a raging mind. But make no mistake: this kind of comfortable isn't some limited state of mind and not some other state of mind. Such limited comfort as that is unreliable.

Sitting in this freefall expresses vast not-knowing—beyond-knowing—of this single dimensionless point that is all things, the one bright pearl of the universe. We might call this *endarkenment* of the universe beyond all seeing—and this endarkenment is a synonym for enlightenment. Sitting amid endarkenment is not limited to any form of experience, any set of circumstances arising, but can meet all that arises, continuously and seamlessly.

And so Dogen tells us: "This is not only practice while

sitting, it is like a hammer striking emptiness: before and after, its exquisite peal permeates everywhere." After all, if it is the fullness of our lives, and of all lives, "How can it be limited to this moment?" he asks. Done correctly, it is the antidote to our false sense of separation. Done correctly, shikantaza reveals who we really are in the fullness of our lives. This is true when sitting, but also in every activity of our lives from child rearing to working.

This is silent illumination. This is our endarkenment and our enlightenment. This is just sitting. This is bearing witness. This is true entrusting. This is Zen meditation.

## 10

# Introducing the Koan

SPIRITUAL PRACTICES based within silence are used in every religion. The koan is the unique gift of the Zen Way. The word is Japanese. It comes from the Chinese *gongan* and translates literally as "public case," as in a legal document. It is a term of art within the Zen community.

However, there are many other uses for the word. A Zen friend referred to a deep question he was pondering as an "honest koan." I had no idea what that "honest" was supposed to mean. What's a dishonest koan? Then it dawned on me he wasn't referring to koan in its spiritual sense at all. And it set me to thinking, once again, about how the word has been transformed within American English. He, and a host of others, including Zen teachers who've not engaged in the discipline of koan introspection, have come to use the word *koan* to stand for "a particularly thorny question." Actually, I've even seen koan downgraded to a simple synonym for "a question" or perhaps a "riddle."

In several senses, it's not wrong to say a koan is a "question," or a "particularly thorny question," or even a "riddle." First, language is mutable; words shift and change and are put to new uses. No problem there. However, one does need to be careful and mindful of the word's meaning when we use it. We don't live in the world of Humpty Dumpty, where a "word means just what I choose it to mean."

Koan also has some particular meanings within the Zen tradition, well beyond a question, or even a thorny question. The American Zen master Robert Aitken suggests a koan is "a matter to be made clear." Elsewhere he calls it a "universal particular." I've found these definitions the most useful of many attempts by many people to define *koan* beyond its etymology and more deeply than its popular use within our contemporary Western culture. I add my own definition: a koan points to something of deep importance and invites us to stand in that place.

No one is precisely sure where koans as a spiritual discipline come from. Josh Bartok points to an intriguing comment in Karen Armstrong's *The Great Transformation: The Beginning of Our Religious Traditions*. Referring to the description of the *brahmodya* ritual in the Rig Veda, arguably the oldest sacred scripture in the world, Armstrong writes,

The challenger asked a difficult and enigmatic question, and his opponent answered in an equally elusive manner. The match continued until one of the contestants was unable to respond: reduced to silence, he was forced to withdraw.

We can, if nothing else, see this as an intriguing example of using words as a spiritual discipline.

As to the koan in Zen, the first things to emerge are the stories that so many feature. They were originally created as part of the hagiographic tradition of the emergent Zen school, where the biographies of the masters were collected along with brief anecdotes of their sayings and doings.

An example is the story of Deshan Xuanjian's visit with Longtan Chongxin. They met in the master's room and discussed the matters of life and death well into the night. Finally, the old teacher said, "It's time for you to retire." So Deshan made his bows and opened the door, but saw it was too dark to walk safely. He turned to the master and said, "It's dark outside." And so Longtan prepared a paper candle and handed it to the young monk. As Deshan took the candle, the old man leaned in and blew the candle out. What we make of that moment is the heart of the koan.

The early influences that led to the final form and use of

koans is not entirely clear. Scholar Steven Heine suggests one possibility. He notes that the spiritual discipline and an early form of detective fiction shared the same name, *gong'an*, derived from the legal term for a public document.

Some of these mysteries, featuring Judge Dee and Magistrate Pao, are translated into English. As a fan of the mystery genre, I personally find this delightful. And certainly the idea of a deep investigation that could be either a murder mystery or the ultimate matter of the human heart conveys degrees of nuance worth considering.

The scholar and Zen priest Victor Sogen Hori suggests a more probable origin for koan practice. He believes this style of engagement may have its origins within medieval Daoist drinking games. While lubricated with copious amounts of wine, someone starts a poem and then someone else must "match it" in a way acceptable to all concerned.

Intriguingly, the American Zen priest Zenshin Florence Caplow once witnessed something similar in a tavern while visiting the ancient city of Chania on Crete. A man sang a spontaneously composed verse. Another man across the room then stood and, locking eyes with the first man, sang another line. Those watching the contest judged with their hoots and laughter whether the match was true. So it seems this form of matching lines of poetry or song is not without precedent in world culture.

Koan practice began with collected anecdotes of the ancestors' words and actions. Then it quickly became discussions and literary reflection. And from there it is an easy step to a playful meeting of those anecdotes by old hands on the Way. Here the stories began to meld with other emerging meditative disciplines, becoming Zen's unique contribution to the world's spiritual treasure trove.

Critical to this was bringing in the Chinese terms *wu-nien,* "no-thought," and *wu-hsien,* "no-mind," as pointers for our common understanding of original awakening. *Wu-nien* is a cutting through all forms of intellectualism to the heart of the matter. Here the distinctions between "my story" and the stories of the ancients begin to inform each other.

Embracing these stories as part of our own personal and intimate insight opens us. On the one hand, it is an invitation into the intimate truths of our ancestors—and on the other hand, it calls us directly into our own experience. The invitation is to something intimate.

Here we are invited to see how everything is as it is, and at the same time how all those things are empty, boundless. We are invited to let go of clinging to any idea of substance and instead find the reality of what is presenting. The Platform Sutra tells us: "Thought after thought is nonabiding. Previous thoughts, present thoughts, and future thoughts continue along, thought after thought—without being cut off or interrupted. . . . If successive thoughts do not abide in any dharma, then this is 'freedom from bondage.'" And so the discipline of koan introspection began to form.

As Robert Buswell observes:

The distinctive rhetoric of Chan developed in tandem with a new pedagogical style, pioneered by Mazu and Linji. This nonconceptual, illocutionary style of teaching—by beating, shouting, or virtually any other kind of physical gesture, in order to rouse students from complacency and catalyze their enlightenment.

Buswell provides a delightful illustration with the famous story of Baizhang walking along a path with his teacher Mazu. They startle a flock of geese, who fly up and off into the sky. Mazu asks, apparently innocently, "What is that?"

To which his student replies, also innocently, "Wild geese."

The old teacher, I imagine, leans in and asks, "Where did they go?"—eliciting the most innocent of answers.

"They flew away," says Baizhang. Mazu then grabs his student by the nose, and gives it a twist.

"How could they have flown away? They've been here from the beginning of all things."

With the pain—and the geese that were gone and never

gone—Baizhang had his first great insight. Even today, if you meet with a Zen teacher and discuss the case and one's own experience, you might want to watch your nose!

OFTEN KOANS would take a literary turn. Here the response would generate some great poetry and inspire other artistic endeavors. This continues to be a part of the koan enterprise—and for both good and ill it is a part of the danger of koan introspection.

The danger lies in how easy it is to turn from the raw, authentic, deeper matters of the heart to a distancing by making it a polished expression. Sometimes that polished expression is indeed our authentic presentation—often, though, the intimate is lost with that generous application of polish.

By the beginning of the eleventh century, Fenyang Shan-chao had compiled three collections of one hundred cases. According to Ruth Fuller Sasaki these became a model for how koans were later compiled and edited, including commentaries, responses, and appreciations. Then, by the twelfth century, the great anthologies began to appear—most notable among them the *Gateless Gate*, *Blue Cliff Record*, and *Book of Serenity*.

The various scholars who have taken up the subject of koan introspection often seem like the blind men exploring an elephant. In the Buddha's illustration, each scholar examines only the part of the elephant near at hand and thinks it represents the whole. As Victor Hori writes, these scholars explore "Zen's nondual epistemology, its ritual and performance, its language, [or] its politics." Some point to the shortcomings of Zen institutions, while others examine how koan study can be abused or misused. And all of these examinations no doubt speak to one truth or another—but none of these considerations alone, nor any several of them, capture the heart that is koan introspection.

## 11

# Doubt and the *Huatou*

IN EARLY BUDDHISM, doubt is simply seen as one of the five hindrances to meditative progress, along with sensual desire, ill will, sloth, and restlessness. In this analysis, doubt is a not-useful pattern of thought, an obstruction to sustained concentration. The principal fix for this was to observe doubt as it rises. This attenuates its power, both in the moment and when it arises again in the future.

This perspective on doubt continues as Buddhism spreads to China. In his concise essay "The Transformation of Doubt in Kanhwa Son," Robert Buswell studies the first Chinese compendium on Buddhist meditation, Kumarajiva's "Book on Sitting Meditation." In this late-fourth- or early-fifth-century work, doubt is still viewed as a detriment, and the prescribed cure is to meditate on dependent origination.

However, in the Zen schools, the use of doubt becomes a central tactic. In fact, in an important way, it becomes the very heart of koan practice. Buswell describes doubt as a sense, feeling, or experience—"a palpable, conative sensation"—adding that it "ultimately serves to pervade all of one's thoughts, feelings, emotions, and eventually even one's physical body." Attending to this sensation becomes the source of continuing energy for engagement.

Buswell speculates that this change of perspective is another of those shifts that came with Buddhism becoming Chinese. However, the shift came about slowly. Master Yuanwu Keqin is a signal figure in the development of koan introspection as it emerges from a literary examination into a meditative discipline. When he writes in the early twelfth century, he still considers doubt in the classical sense as a hindrance.

Within a generation, Yuanwu Keqin's renowned disciple Dahui Zonggao makes doubt central in Zen practice. It is Dahui who sees the utility of allowing doubt to drive us forward.

Today the form of koan practice most common in China and Korea is *huatou*. The modern Chan master Sheng Yen trained both in China and Japan. He was uniquely familiar with Chinese huatou disciplines, as well as both the Japanese Rinzai and Harada-Yasutani reform approaches to the koan curriculum.

Master Sheng Yen observed that the difference between a koan and a huatou is that koans require an answer—while there is never an answer in huatou practice. Instead, we're invited into the mind before the question fully formulates. I suspect this Chinese and Korean discipline reflects the oldest form of koan introspection practice.

My old friend, a Dharma bum who goes by his Native American name Weasel Tracks, is also a longtime practitioner of the huatou discipline. In an exchange of emails he lists some standard questions one might take up: "What is *Wu*?" (*Wu* is *mu* in Chinese.) "Who is dragging this corpse around?" "Who am I?" "What was my original face before my parents were born?" "Who is reciting Buddha's name?" (This latter practice is recommended several times in *The Chan Whip Anthology* for Pure Land practitioners.) A particular favorite of the great modern Korean master Kusan Sunim was "It is not the body. It is not the mind. What is it?"

As with Japanese-style koan introspection, each of these huatou are "identity" questions. They point, return, drag, whisper, and shout to the meditator the abiding secret of the Zen Way. They guide us to who and what we are, to our true identity. As the practitioner holds the word or phrase in her or his mind, they are invited to dig into and explore the phrase in any way they can imagine.

Stephen Batchelor—who, before gaining fame and notoriety as a Buddhist atheist, studied as a monk for four years in the Tibetan tradition and then for four more years with the Korean

Zen master Kusan Sunim—writes that the kind of doubt spoken of in Zen "should be thought of as a psychosomatic condition of astonishment and bafflement rather than as a discursive mental process."

Another helpful way to phrase this is that we are invited into curiosity—digging, not unlike a small child asking *why, why, why, why?* Except with koans, the meditator is both the small child asking and the adult hearing the question. In this way, we are invited to engage the actual questions of our lives. Why are we here? What is the meaning of my life? What will become of me? Such are some of the core questions that can drive the spiritual quest.

And at some point there is *only* the question—and there has always only been one question. We may frame it differently, we may use an "artificial" form of the question, something given to us as a koan or huatou, but it is meant only to open our hearts to our deepest longing. Exploring that question is an invitation to follow that longing down to the bottom.

Following it that way eventually reveals everything. You find who you are. You discover what the universe is. Insights, small and large, come like a gentle rain, or in a torrent. We can actually know our individual reality and its tenuousness as only a moment within a great causal dance.

We can know in a sense vastly deeper than the words

themselves can convey. The poets speak of knowing in our bones and marrow, and stepping away from self and other. Pursuing the huatou down to the bottom, we often are gifted with flashes of that experience. Actually even the word *experience* can't quite capture it in all its fullness.

These experiences are both private and shared, and because of that, "right" answers appear for koans. In many koan cases, one answer is obvious to anyone with the perspective discovered in this practice. In most cases, there are various options that all work. But anyone who has delved deeply into the matter can "see" why someone would emphasize some particular answer—and how courses of study can emerge using the koans one after another, each with "correct" and "wrong" responses.

## 12

# Great Doubt, Great Faith, Great Determination

ZEN PRACTICE requires three things, whether using koans or not: Great Doubt, Great Faith, and Great Determination. These points were developed and expanded from Dahui's exhortation to doubt, by the thirteenth-century Linji master Gaofeng Yuanmiao. As Master Gaofeng (as translated in Robert Buswell's essay "The Transformation of Doubt") tells us, if we're speaking about authentic Zen contemplation:

There have to be three essentials. The first essential is to have the faculty of great faith: This matter should be so patently obvious that it is just as if you are leaning against Mt. Sumeru. The second essential is to have great fury, which is just as if you've come across the villain who murdered your father and right then and there you want to cut him in half with a single strike of your sword. The third essential is to have the sensation of great doubt, which is just as if you've done a heinous act in secret and are about to be exposed.

These "essentials" are more commonly presented as those three pillars of Zen practice: Great Faith, Great Doubt, and Great Energy or Determination (or even Courage). As we dig into this as a living practice, I find a lot in Professor Buswell's translation of that Great Determination or Courage as "fury."

Don't confuse Great Doubt with skeptical doubt. This is a spiritual call to question authority, both external and, equally, our own. When we start looking into how we engage the world, we quickly realize the highest authority in our lives is the one inside our skulls. This authority tells us all sorts of things—and, frankly, it is a liar. It speaks sometimes in a whisper, sometimes a shout: perhaps that we're the greatest—or, just as popular, we're the worst.

Turning doubt on ourselves, questioning each thought that arises, we strive to manifest that bumper-sticker truth: "Don't believe everything you think." However, the invitation here is even more radical: Don't believe *anything* you think.

Of course there's still faith. All those years ago I asked Jiyu-Kennett Roshi how much faith I needed to undertake serious

Zen practice. She replied that I only needed to believe that there might possibly be some use in practicing Zen. In some sense, our faith need be no more than what the Jewish sage compared to a mustard seed, "the smallest of things."

It doesn't take much faith to begin a spiritual practice like Zen—and for this I'm grateful, because faith doesn't come naturally to me. All one really needs to begin this practice is a feeling that something positive *might* come of it. It is a belief, yes. And there is nothing particularly "objective" compelling this belief. However, there doesn't need to be. It can be nothing more than a vague hope. Which, truthfully, is about all I had when I began. If you're willing to suspend disbelief to even this degree, it's enough.

Quickly, however, if we take on the discipline and open our hearts and minds to the practice, things happen. We quickly have intimations that enlarge our sense of confidence in this project, our growing faith. This evolving faith, found within an engagement with doubt, becomes Great Faith. And it deserves those capital letters. It is our growing openness to what is, and our growing confidence in what we encounter. Great Faith starts as curiosity and blossoms into a dynamic engagement, a dance of the soul.

In koan introspection, doubt and faith travel together. Each informs the other. It is our relentless presence to doubt and faith that takes us to the gate of nondual insight. Indeed, both the path to the gate and the gate itself are discovered within that relentlessness, that willingness to not turn away. This relentlessness is Great Determination.

From an instrumentalist view of koan introspection, words like *Mu* or phrases like "What is the sound of the single hand?" or "What is your original face from before your parents were born?" are often mistakenly assumed to be meaningless. It is assumed that the "point" of such koans is to simply startle the discursive mind into some kind of transrational state. But this understanding of koans simply posits a new dualism: a lower discursive consciousness and a higher nondiscursive state. This dividing is not what koan introspection is about. We seek to cut the two into one.

As we push through Great Doubt, Great Faith, and Great Determination in our koan practice, we find the exact identity between our ordinary consciousness and our fundamental openness. Nondual reality includes subject and object, each itself and freely transposing with the other.

First this, now that. Sometimes one drops away, sometimes the other, sometimes both drop away, sometimes one emerges from the other, sometimes both emerge together. But we rest nowhere. Resting nowhere and moving fluidly among these perspectives is the true practice of koan introspection.

Koan study, koan introspection, begins with a step reminiscent of that original way in. The beginning student is given a "breakthrough" koan, a case specifically meant to elicit an initial experience of nonduality. The Japanese term for this koan is *shokan*, or "first barrier." A student might spend years struggling with it, although occasionally someone passes through the breakthrough koan quickly. One never knows.

Most commonly this breakthrough koan is Zhaozhou's *Mu*. The set up is simplicity itself. A student of the Way comes to Zhaozhou and asks, "Does a dog have buddha nature?"

Zhaozhou replies, "Mu."

*Mu* means "no." But to leave it at that is making a mistake. The modern Rinzai master Keido Fukushima informs us, "Mu doesn't just have a negative meaning; Mu doesn't just refer to nothing. Mu means 'although it is, it isn't, and although it isn't, it is.'" From the beginning therefore there is a curious, challenging, internally contradictory invitation—to something.

Mu, as we've learned, is one of the central options for those who engage huatou practice. In koan introspection, Mu has become the most commonly used of all the various potential opening cases.

Even without Fukushima Roshi's enigmatic definition hanging in the air, there is a lot buried within the above exchange. The conversation takes place near the beginning of the ninth century in China, where a dog was considered vermin. So does a rat have buddha nature? Does the AIDS virus have buddha nature? Does a person holding political views you abhor have buddha nature?

We can assume the student is an old hand and knows the "doctrinally correct" answer is of course that a dog has buddha nature. Or, more correctly, a dog is a part of buddha nature. Or— even more precisely—dogs and buddha nature are one thing.

We can also assume we have no monopoly on low self-esteem. The student is asking about herself, about himself.

"No" is an invitation. In this practice everything is thrown away except that single sound: *Mu*. It is the first case collected in Wumen Huikai's *Wumenguan*, the *Gateless Gate*, and Master Wumen offers a short sermon with it, translated by Koun Yamada. It is worth reading.

For the practice of Zen, you must pass the barrier set up by the ancient patriarchs of Zen. To attain to marvelous enlightenment, you must completely extinguish all thoughts of the ordinary mind. If you have not passed the barrier and have not extinguished all thoughts, you are a phantom haunting the weeds and trees. Now, just tell me, what is the barrier set up by the patriarchs? Merely this Mu—the one barrier of our sect. So it has come to be called "The Gateless Barrier of the Zen Sect."

Those who have passed the barrier are able not only to see Zhaozhou face to face but also to walk hand in hand with the whole descending line of patriarchs and be eyebrow to eyebrow with them. You will see with the same eye that they see with, hear with the same ear that they hear with. Wouldn't it be a wonderful joy? Isn't there anyone who wants to pass this barrier? Then concentrate your whole self into this Mu, making your whole body with its 360 bones and joints and 84,000 pores into a solid lump of doubt. Day and night, without ceasing, keep digging into it, but don't take it as "nothingness" or as "being" or "non-being." It must be like a red-hot iron ball which you have gulped down and which you try to vomit up but cannot. You must extinguish all delusive thoughts and beliefs that you have cherished up to the present. After a certain period of such efforts, Mu will come to fruition, and inside and out will become one naturally. You will then be like a dumb man who has had a dream.

You will know yourself and for yourself only. Then all of a sudden, Mu will break open. It will astonish the heavens and shake the earth. It will be just as if you had snatched the great sword of General Kuan: If you meet a Buddha, you will kill him. If you meet a patriarch, you will kill him. Though you may stand on the brink of life and death, you will enjoy the great freedom. In the six realms and the four modes of birth, you will live in the samadhi of innocent play.

Now, how should you concentrate on Mu? Exhaust every ounce of energy you have in doing it. And if you do not give up on the Way, you will be enlightened the way a candle in front of the altar is lighted by one touch of fire.

Did I mention how, out of necessity, one is given insufficient instructions for working with Mu? So there isn't a lot more the student can grab on to. One might be advised to "become Mu." One might be asked to mentally wash that Mu through everything one encounters. One might be asked if there is anything that is not Mu? Oh, maybe one hint. Zen teacher Melissa Myozen Blacker points out how this no, Mu, "is not the opposite of anything."

# 13

# Mu All the Way Down

A FEW YEARS AGO I edited an anthology on the koan Mu with the Zen teacher Melissa Myozen Blacker. There I noted how much I love Wumen's little sermon on Mu. He evokes a lively practice and calls us to the importance of finding our own way into the Great Matter.

And there should be no doubt, this project is as important as can be. This practice really is about life and death—and it's not some abstract idea of life and death. It is about our lived lives, our actual deaths, yours and mine. The old master gets it right down to his bones and marrow, and he conveys it eloquently.

There is no doubt that many of us encounter the koan as a red-hot iron ball. Particularly within the context of retreat where there are few other distractions, the question, the word, the noise Mu can become the holder for all the burning questions of life, rendered into this one thing. Mu. And hot is surely how that is encountered.

Blacker tells us:

On the surface Zhaozhou's Mu is a simple dialogue between two human beings. When we first begin working with this koan, we must dive under the surface of its apparent meaning and possibly our own confusions about it. Our relationship with the koan begins when we start to deeply wonder.

That "wonder" gives us another angle on the word *doubt*. It has several possible names, maybe *wonder*, *hesitation*, or perhaps *concern*. However we call it, this is the magic element. Questions surround the koan, bubble from within it, seem to hover above it. Is this koan even useful? What is it, really? Is it a mantra? Should I repeat it over and over? Is it a way to breathe? Is it a metaphor for something? And if so, what is that something? And how am I supposed to relate to that something, whatever it might be?

Doubt, wonder, hesitation, concern—questions piling upon questions. Zen teacher David Rynick says, "the point of Mu, and the point of Buddhism, is not to get rid of our capacity to think and plan, but rather to see through it so thoroughly that we are no longer held in its thrall."

Wumen has thrown out a snare for the unwary. It is also

true that for many of us, that red-hot iron ball isn't at all how Mu is encountered. Mu can be confusion itself. Neither burning hot nor freezing cold, just confusion. Mu can be a nagging something in the back of your head. Mu can be a small pebble in your shoe. Mu can become the longing inhabiting your dreams, emerging in so many unlikely ways. And Mu can be encountered like a blueberry found on a bush. You just reach out, pick it, and throw it into your mouth.

It can be any of these things. And more.

I've repeated the following anecdote before, as I find it particularly inspiring, and feel it speaks to the heart of our Way. I have a friend who, many years before she took up the Zen Way, was canoeing alone in Maine's far northern wilderness. Let's call her Georgia.

Georgia dipped her paddle into the water, and in that moment she was struck, first by the sound of a small splash, then by the feel of resistance as the paddle slipped deeper into the water, then by the smells of water and air and canoe. Everything seemed so clean, with little connection to the experiences of her life back in Boston.

Georgia was startled into silence. In that silence all that was left was the flow of life itself, a flock of geese, the clouds overhead, the splash of some fish, and that crisp smell.

The moment passed quickly enough, but some part of her

never forgot. It seemed as if it were some small secret she and the universe shared. Time passed and things happened. There was a divorce. There were changes in work.

Georgia felt dissatisfaction with her life and who she had become, and wanted to find her way again. She thought what she needed was a spiritual discipline. She began to meditate in the Zen style and ended up in one of our sanghas.

Early on she came in for an interview. We talked about life and practice and her hopes and we agreed that settling down and just noticing might be good for her. Georgia took up the practice of breath counting. After she had been sitting a while counting her breath, perhaps for seven or eight months, she realized that the koan way might be a right next step for her. And so, as is our usual practice in Boundless Way, she was presented with Mu. She made her bows and left.

Some months later Georgia came to sesshin. A day or so into it she came into dokusan and said to me, "You know, James. I'm not sure why, but Mu for me is that moment of silence I experienced all those years ago, but made fresh. Instead of honking geese and the smell of forest air, it's the roar of that car which just drove down the road and that funny off-white color of the wall."

And she said one other thing. All of this caught my attention. We pursued the matter further. I asked her one of the usual checking questions. And she knew the answer. I asked another, and another, and she kept meeting them fully.

Here's the point. Georgia never had the red-hot iron ball experience. She didn't need it. For her, Mu was found like a flower opening, as gentle as gentle can be.

WHAT WE'RE PROMISED by the teachers of our Way is that we and all things, you and I, and every blessed thing, share the same root. Mu is just a noise. It is a placeholder. But what it holds for us is a way of being in the world. It's always here. We just don't notice it.

The catch is that the other way of being in the world, of slicing and dicing, of separating and weighing and judging, well, it's important. It's useful. In fact, seeing into our shared place isn't particularly useful.

It doesn't pay the bills. It doesn't get us a girlfriend or a boyfriend. It's in fact the most counter-cultural thing we can be about. And so, even though we are surrounded by it, we miss it. Its very existence slips into the back of our human consciousness. And even though it is the background of our lives, we forget it.

It is our common heritage, our birthright as we enter into this universe. It peeks out at us in our dreams. It whispers to us in the dark. It beckons in the playing of children and the touch of a kiss. And it appears even in some very rough patches of our lives, sometimes the roughest. You never know when it will present.

# 14

# Curricular Koan Study

By MOST ACCOUNTS, as koan introspection developed as a discipline, a list of specific "answers" were collected. Eventually (and problematically), these answers came to be imparted ritually to chosen students. The literary level of koans led people to take a solely intellectual and artistic path rather than follow the matter of our heart's longing right down to the bottom. As this happened, the practice of koan study waned in popularity over the centuries. Its most important revival came with Hakuin in eighteenth-century Japan.

It seems likely that people were studying a succession of koans at least as early as the composition of the great koan anthologies, although it is not clear precisely how these might have been engaged. But following Hakuin, some Japanese Rinzai Zen teachers began introducing koan "curricula." These were programs of koan study through which a student "passed" during the course of many years. These were closely associated with Hakuin and his principal students and their successors.

This program is used within Japanese Rinzai to this day. There are two major variations, the Takujo and the Inzan lines. Of particular importance for us in the West is the Harada-Yasutani curriculum, the Takujo-derived modern reform system used in some Soto schools.

The Japanese Soto master Daiun Sogaku Harada initiated a reform movement within the Soto school in the early twentieth century. After a period of training with several Rinzai masters, including Dokutan Sosan, he developed a simplified form of the Hakuin/Takujo curriculum.

Harada left two significant lines of transmission, one within the Soto school and the other through his disciple, the priest Haku'un Yasutani. Yasutani formed a lay organization named Sanbo Kyodan (Order of the Three Treasures), renamed Sanbo Zen in recent years. This form of curricular koan practice is the one most frequently encountered in the West. And it is the form of koan introspection that has become the heart of my own spiritual life.

In the West, there is also another systematized curriculum taught by successors of the Korean master Seung Sahn in the Kwan Um School. It resembles the Japanese Rinzai curricular koan style in many ways, although it has distinctive features. One of the Kwan Um teachers told me she believed it was an indigenous Korean approach to koans—but I can't find any reference in Korean Zen to koan work other than the huatou practice. We know that Seung Sahn was closely associated for a time with Yanase Roshi, a Japanese Rinzai master. And Master Seung Sahn spent time in Japan itself where he had ample opportunity to encounter teachers of the Japanese style. Beyond that, my sense of the history of the master's approach is all speculation.

Whatever its origins, this Kwan Um curriculum reflects the power of the huatou practice with which Master Seung Sahn began his own path of inquiry. The master's *Ten Gates: The Kong-an Teaching of Zen Master Seung Sahn* provides a solid introduction to his approach. And Richard Shrobe, one of his successors, wrote a book called *Elegant Failure: A Guide to Zen Koans*, which shows how this style of koan introspection does indeed open the heart in all its mysterious and powerful ways.

The lists of koans is quite long; the traditional number totals them at seventeen hundred. This figure is partly mythical, according to Jeff Shore, Zen teacher and professor at Hanazono University. He says that number actually comes from the list of people in Chingde's *Transmission of the Flame*.

Within curricular koan Zen, one might examine a great many more cases than seventeen hundred. Professor Shore notes one lineage tradition that appears to ask some three thousand. Most koan introspection lists include somewhere in the vicinity of four to six hundred cases. However, each koan may include many points of encounter, which could be counted. And often they are.

In any case, one encounters a lot of koans in this introspection practice. It takes ten, twenty, thirty, forty years to work through them for most of us. I practiced with them for a little shy of twenty years before they were truly my bones and marrow.

# 15

# Koan Introspection in the West

Koans may teach us in many ways, and there are dangers that come along with that wide possible use. At its nadir point in the past, koan introspection became ritualized with rote responses. Practitioners were given, or sometimes even procured on their own, the "answers." Even today it is possible to purchase collections of koans and responses, some of which are recognizable by those of us who practice within the tradition.

Reformers came along and cleared out the temple, starting nearly all over again. Hakuin Ekaku is a prime example of such a reformer coming at an exactly right time. Daiun Sogaku Harada is another.

I've read scholars who have followed koans very deeply into the weeds, to the point where their utility as a spiritual discipline is very, very hard to find. And I've seen people fetishize koans as akin to something delivered from the gods—which should never, ever be used in any but a tightly prescribed manner. They create idols of the mind, if not the heart. It's hardly surprising that the rise of the koan has been both lauded as an amazing gift and decried as final evidence of the decline of the Dharma.

In Japan, the school of Zen most associated with koan study is the Rinzai school. For complicated reasons the Rinzai school has not yet taken significant root outside of Japan. The training available in the West has not included, as near as I can ascertain, the full traditional Rinzai koan training. A couple of Westerners have trained in Japan; I'm aware of two who have completed the formal curriculum within the mainstream schools. I believe only one is fully authorized to teach. Other Rinzai teachers who offer koan training seem to use the Harada-Yasutani reform curriculum or a similarly modified one.

Here in the West the whole koan enterprise seems to be experiencing a reset. We have been gifted with the barest tools, a solid list of cases, and some guidance on how to work with them. And today there are any number of people who are competent to guide people along the koan way.

But the very system within which we work is itself a work in progress. Our style lacks many elements considered essential in the Japanese Rinzai school. For instance, the Japanese style includes *jakugo* (capping phrases). This practice takes literary tags from East Asian culture, which must then be matched with a particular koan. Capping phrases are a major undertaking, potentially adding years to formal curricular koan study.

Victor Hori describes how powerfully traditional capping phrases complement koan introspection in the Japanese Rinzai system, an essential checking process. So while they are not essential to fully engage koan introspection, their elimination in most Western curricula is nonetheless a loss. For a comprehensive exploration, I highly recommend Hori's *Zen Sand: The Book of Capping Phrases for Koan Practice.*

It remains to be seen how our Western Zen schools will replace this rigorous practice. Capping phrases are absent in the Harada-Yasutani system, and aren't much used in American Rinzai either. However, it is possible to adapt them, and some Western Rinzai teachers do use capping phrases. I can imagine a Western set of literary tags, or a combination drawing upon the world's literature emerging as our own Western Zen koan disciplines mature.

# 16

# Meeting the Koan

So what does one encounter in a koan?

Over the years people with a little time on their hands have attempted to categorize koans. The oldest categorization in Japan, probably tracing to China, is three-fold: *richi*, ultimate truth; *kikan*, devices; and *kojo*, reality itself. According to William Bodiford, these seem to correspond to classical presentations of enlightenment as nature, function, and appearance. Master Hakuin suggested five categories.

*Hosshin* or *dharmakaya* koans address the full body of the Buddha, the nondual. Mu and koans such as Hakuin's "Sound of the Single Hand" are classic examples.

*Kikan* koans express action arising out of the empty, with "Nanchuan Cuts the Cat" and "Oak Tree in the Garden" as examples. (The koans referenced here as examples here appear as an appendix to this book.)

*Gonsen* koans are the explication or skillful use of words, like

"Every Day Is a Good Day" and "Wash Your Bowls."

Next are *nanto* koans, the extremely difficult cases. Examples of these are Wuzu's "Ox's Tail" and the "Old Woman Burns Down the Hut."

Last are the *goi* koans. Dongshan's five ranks or five modes, which we'll discuss later, as well as the precepts treated as koans are of this type.

For others there are more or fewer categories. The American Rinzai priest Genjo Marinello observes how the various koans can be placed in one or another of Dongshan's famous five ranks. I've found that useful.

But for our purposes here, I suggest simply looking at them as fitting within three categories. First, koans that are concerned with helping us find our place within our original boundlessness. Second, koans that explore various aspects of boundlessness and particularity in the great dance that is our lives. And third, koans that open us to the many realities of our hearts, to a dynamic, mysterious reality. I will return to this threefold list later.

Professor Shore says that all koans, however else they might be defined, can also be seen as "problem, challenge, probe, and as expression." In our lives, we have any number of problems that capture our attention. These questions drive us into the spiritual quest and often are the shape of spiritual quest itself. Here we find the heart of the huatou and of koans.

And here we experience the rising of doubt—which is Professor Shore's "challenge." Living into this dynamically, however it takes shape, is the "probe." Every action that follows is the "expression."

As an example, he uses the encounter between Bodhidharma and Dazu Huike, who would become Bodhidharma's successor. In this koan from the *Gateless Gate*, Huike declares he is "not at peace." Here is a clear example of the problem of the human heart, the challenge. This is followed with the question, "What do I do?" And the master says, "Bring me that 'I'"—in other words, show me your true self—"and I will put it at ease."

This question, "Who am I?" burns in many hearts. I encounter it in the interview room, framed in all sorts of ways. It is not necessary to use the old stories, but there is something about them that actually helps us. Seeing ourselves in these ancient encounters can be an authentic way to get into the matter.

"My mind, my heart is not at peace," and the invitation, "bring me this mind, this heart," is the very heart of koan introspection. I never cease to feel gratitude when this invitation is accepted and the koan "resolves." We probe the various aspects of the answer as well as the question. And then how do we bring it all into manifestation?

Koans can be defined with even more granularity than this. For instance, Hakuin in his fivefold list introduced what he called *nanto*, which seems to translate best as "unbelievably hard" koan. He identified eight specific examples. Hori seems to have found ten or so of the "eight."

One Zen master suggested these eight or ten or whatever were simply those particularly difficult *for Hakuin*. I can guarantee we all will have our own particular *nanto*, custom-designed by the universe just for us.

Or as the old Zen hand Jan Seymour-Ford observes, "our clinging is customized just for the koans." Again, there is something compelling in how elusive it all can be. This is powerful stuff. It is about who we really are. It is about the ways we are trapped and how we can win our freedom.

I hope, while koan becomes an English synonym for thorny problems, we don't forget these are also an invitation from our ancestors to look deeply into our hearts. To look to the place where all questions arise and where all questions, at least those of meaning and purpose, of who and what we are, may be resolved.

I mentioned in passing how koans have been used as the subject for conversations. Although the modern Soto school does not practice koan introspection, many Soto teachers use koans as subjects for talks and discussion within small groups.

In fact, the Japanese Soto school seems to have had a flourishing koan introspection tradition well into the sixteenth century. According to Shore the style was somewhat different, with an emphasis more on probe-expression than problem-challenge, to use his model. And so in some of these traditional Soto lines, the "answers" might be given with the koan itself. But the challenge remains deep and profound.

The full value of the koan is to be found in how it is lived into. I can't emphasize this point too strenuously. It is critical if we want to understand the koan way.

Of course, this is all a human discipline. And it is subject to clumsy use and misuse, abuse, simple misunderstanding.

The amount of nonsense written about enlightenment, about awakening in Zen, fills libraries. (Perhaps you can find examples in your personal library . . .) With all of this, be careful. Being able to separate wheat from chaff can take years. Fortunately we don't exactly have to, and certainly not as an intellectual endeavor. The invitation is into the living experience of koan introspection, and this invitation is extended by way of a breakthrough koan like Mu.

In fact Mu isn't the only possible question that works in such a way. "What was your face before your parents were born?" is another. "Stop that distant temple bell" can work quite nicely. But, here I find myself thinking of what probably is the most widely known koan outside of the Zen tradition.

The eighteenth-century Japanese master Hakuin Ekaku asks it directly: "We've all heard the sound of two hands clapping. What is the sound of the single hand?"

The oldest reference I can find to that single hand is collected in the *Biyan Lu*, the *Blue Cliff Record*. In a commentary on case 18, "The National Teacher's Seamless Tomb," written perhaps a hundred years before it was collected into the anthology, the master Xuedou Zhongxian says, "The single palm of the hand does not make a sound in vain."

But it is Hakuin who turns it into the koan. For many it is a nonsense statement. Or a conundrum similar to that question "If a tree falls in the forest and there is no one to hear it, is there a sound?"

People here in the West have played with it over the years. A couple of years ago, I was watching an episode of *The Simpsons* in which Bart gives Lisa his "understanding" by flapping his fingers onto the palm of his hand, producing a faint clapping sound. In some sense, it's not such a bad response; it shows the playfulness that koans often inspire. But this is very serious play, play that illuminates the Great Matter.

Koans are actually about life and death. They are about our lives and our deaths, in the most intimate sense. They are about who we are, you and I, about our true home, about what it is to be human and present to what is. Present to all that is.

With a breakthrough koan we encounter what some call the nondual. We're invited to step away from clinging to either self or other. In the terminology of Zen, the question is an invitation into the Great Matter.

And we need to bring everything into it—Great Doubt, Great Faith, and Great Determination, even to the point of fury. It demands our full attention. Whatever the form, we are asked to throw ourselves into the Great Matter wholeheartedly.

Without clear direction we may come at it in any number of ways. At some point we may try critical analysis. At another point, it may become a mantra. It might be chanted, breathed, whispered, yelled. And each time we think we gain some insight, some intimation of what it might mean. And we take it into the interview room where, most probably, our teacher will reject our response.

Yet koan introspection is a dialogistic discipline; it does require a teacher. We dig deep, we find and present our treasure to someone who can distinguish between fool's gold and authentic treasure. But, and this is important, the teacher doesn't *give us* the treasure. She only tests it. He only pushes us to find the real deal. But that real deal, our awakening, is always and has always been ours.

Many teachers along the Way say that awakening comes to us as an accident. And I tell my own students this today: There is no obvious causal relationship between nondual insight and anything we might do or not do. If our awakening is an accident, certain spiritual practices can help us become accident-prone. Koan practice is particularly effective at creating this.

If we open ourselves to this great adventure, eventually it will happen. That bus hits us, and everything changes. With our awakening the world becomes something new and precious. Or perhaps the bus just grazes us as it passes by. But even that graze is valuable.

This is the point of our engaging these practices, of encountering the koan and Zen meditation, in finding the koan of Zen meditation.

# 17

# Some Ways to Miss the Point

WHEN A STUDENT has demonstrated insight into the basic matter, the teacher trained in koan introspection may ask "checking questions." These reveal how nuanced our insight is. In the case of a breakthrough koan, there might be dozens, maybe as many as a hundred, checking questions. For other cases, there are usually several checking questions.

There are problems with a spiritual practice that has "right" answers. Maybe someone told you the answer. In fact, there are a few books that purport to give "answers" to koans. Some of these published responses are even accurate, at least in the sense of listing some of the traditional, classic responses. But so what? The reality is that koans all follow logically from one's initial insight into nonduality.

Occasionally, for reasons that completely elude me, people will present another student's answers to their teacher in the interview room. As if some formal or official "passing" of a koan were somehow the important thing, instead of liberation from our own and the world's suffering.

Because it is a system, you can sometimes think your way into "answers." You can work through the koans. Possibly, although it isn't very likely, you can think your way through all of them. However, it rarely takes many checking questions to reveal the true quality of a student's insight. But, really, what's the point in doing that?

The invitation that has been thrown open for us is to stand in that awakened place. We are being invited to experience awakening for ourselves. Yes, the word *experience* is usually avoided by teachers. Language is a tangle. It can trap, but it can also liberate. That said, the invitation is into our own lives, authentic and raw. The actual heartful practice of koan introspection is about the healing of the great wound. Why would someone waste their time collecting little reassurances for their ego, pretending to be a person on the koan way?

There are actually numerous traps we encounter along the way in koan introspection. In addition to cheating I notice five snares for the unwary. One my grandmother called "being too smart for our britches." Another is rushing along. One more is missing the connections to our lives. Similar to that but sufficiently different to mark out is missing the personal issues that rise with the koan. And last is not integrating what we find into who we are.

That first one from my grandmother means bringing a discursive mind to the project. There is a simple logic to koan introspection. It is about form and emptiness, and the "answers" always arise from that. And so with a small insight, one can guess one's way through the curriculum. I've seen people do that. And it is a terrible waste of an amazing discipline. The invitation is to open our hearts and allow the responses to the questions to present themselves naturally.

And that is closely connected to the warning about rushing along. There is no goal to this project. It isn't about finishing. In fact there is no finishing, well, not until we die—and arguably not even then. But along the way, all along the Way, what we're really about is growing into the real. Growing into what we are and what we can be. Enjoy the moment, fall into the moment, explore and push and dive into the moment. There is in fact nothing else.

Which moves seamlessly into the warning about missing the connections to our lives. Koan introspection is an endlessly faceted invitation into the mess of being human. And a lot more comes with a koan than the "point." We have to engage that point, but we are also being invited to fully inhabit our hearts and minds. And it is a mistake to dismiss the opportunity when it presents. Spend some time with the koan, even if it's more than necessary if we were only looking to pass a test.

Subtly different are those personal issues, the pains of past and present, that can arise with any given koan. The project is not psychological, but it is connected to our psychological healing. We have the opportunity to engage our wounds, not in a wallowing sort of way, but in an opening to the wholeness.

The last mistake on this brief list is not integrating. If we take on this rich practice, we encounter the many parts of who we are. We can dig deep into those places and allow them to flow together into the lovely mess that is ourselves.

In fact the true richness of the practice is found only within the years of engagement. Koan introspection is an offering into a lifetime of ever-greater depth. With diligence, and a little luck, we can follow the vermillion thread all the way.

18

# After Mu

ONE THING I love about curricular koan practice is that the questions keep coming. And, if you persist, things happen. Whether you have actually responded to the question out of your own insight or parroted another's answer, there is always further digging into the matter.

As the Zen teacher Josh Bartok observes, the system is multiply redundant. The questions pile up, one upon another. "They say when you hear the sound of the single hand you become Buddha? How do you become Buddha?" Or, "Show me the sound of the single hand before your parents were born." Or, "What happens to the single hand when you die?"

This is all about our hurt and loss, our longing, and our finding. I've found that Zen in all its variety is about embodiment. Just sitting is an invitation into becoming Buddha. And koan introspection is about embodying awakening, finding it in every action, in every thought. When we engage a koan we're being invited into the mysterious activity that is our real lives in our real bodies.

It is about the grand teachings of form and emptiness as we take our children to school in the morning. It is about the dance of form and emptiness as we walk down the street on a rainy day. Here we find the language of dragons is in fact our original language.

I've found the koan way is an encounter with the enchantment that is our ordinary lives. It has nothing to do with turning away. Rather, it is all about finding our true joy. And equally important, it is about finding our full sorrow. Koans are one encounter after another, fully expressed within our everyday actions. The process can feel brutal. And sometimes it is. It is after all a dissolution of everything we thought was true, right down to our own sense of self. We examine everything carefully. And then we put all of it together again. It is the same world, but made new and fresh.

When the story of the Buddha was told at the beginning of this book, you may have noticed that the narrative moved into a formal analysis, complete with lists and stages. But as Zen emerged in China, the project moved into metaphor and dream; the disciplines become a dance. And doubt and accident become the heart of the Way.

Historically, the practice of koan introspection is a move

away from the dry structural analysis we find in much of the sutras, or the minute analysis of *Abhidharma*. It is a living spirituality. It is discovering our lives, not as prose but as poetry. As the Zen teacher Desmond Gilna observes, "Rather than speaking of impermanence, we speak of flowers fluttering in the spring breeze. Rather than speaking of nirvana, we speak of the iron ox or the stone maiden." These are pointers, and more, invitations into the moment—living, pulsing, mysterious, terrible, and beautiful.

Zen teacher Dosho Port says this practice is "learning how to enter the koan and make it dance. Actualizing our initial insight in various real-life situations. Bringing it into the interview room to hone the skill of doing it outside the room, making the Zen narrative our own, and making our personal narrative a koan."

And as Aitken Roshi (my own teacher's teacher) would say, "Fine words butter no parsnips." This Way is also difficult. It is a hard practice and can be painful. Often it is terribly painful. Again, as Aitken Roshi observed, "Our practice is not to clear up the mystery. It is to make the mystery clear." We sink into the koan as into a poem, allowing the many different levels of encounter, the various intimacies of our lives their reality, all of them at the same time.

And so the heart of the practice is presentational. From those probably misty origins in Daoist drinking games, the meeting is as often physical as it is verbal. Because we're invited into showing, not explaining. So the project is about laughing, not engaging in a discourse on laughing. It is about showing pain, not writing a paper on the subject. It can feel artificial, particularly at the beginning. And a particular seduction of the ego engaging this practice is to make it all a show. Another danger is for the practice to be reduced to rote. After all, this is a human device, made by people. And it is always subject to abuse.

We wander into the ways of the koans. As Gilna observes, "We become the monk searching for the truth, his angst is our angst; we become the mountain and the valley; we learn to speak from the center that is everywhere, the monk in distress, the layman who falls down followed by his daughter, we become the laughter and the pain; we lose ourselves by stretching the boundary of body so all is embodied."

Me, I've learned from hard experience we are always subject to self-deception. We fall deeply into the practice and it opens us. And, just as easily, we fool ourselves and try to fool others with a fake response. But fortunately and blessedly, the system is, as Bartok told us, "multiply redundant."

We come to the various points over and over. If we fail and give a false response one time, even if it's accepted, we will return to it again. We are given one more chance to make a full and honest presentation. And then another. And another. The lessons are discovered and learned and forgotten and renewed over and over again. The curriculum itself is finite, even if it might seem otherwise when we're in the middle of it. The practice is in fact the work of a lifetime.

As we proceed we lose our false sense of who and what we are, layer by painful layer. We push our near-endless ideas of boundaries, discovering the far territory of intimacy. From the outside it might look like play-acting. But it isn't if we're taking it all with the seriousness the project calls us to.

Perhaps it's best to say curricular koan introspection is deadly serious play. It is the play of life and death, the play of meaning and meaninglessness. It is the play of embodiment. So among the miracles of the discipline is how the practice takes on a shape unique to each of us, to you and me.

Also, I think it is important to hold up that koan introspection isn't for everybody. My koan teacher liked to suggest the smart ones can find their way simply with sitting. He didn't say it, but the traditional Soto way of sitting and attention to form, to detail, is fully the way of embodiment. But the tough cases (and he would then look at me); well, they need koans.

A slightly more generous way of saying this is that each of us has a personal style and each of us will find a way that is useful for us. Within Zen there are two basic practices: sitting in silence, or sitting in silence with a side order of koans. A critical part of the practice is not separating it from just sitting.

The cultivation of samadhi allows us to avoid becoming merely academic or cerebral. So koan introspection is really always sitting *and* koans. Or, as we like to say in Zen, "not one, not two."

EACH OF US will find our own way into the koan. Some of us are aggressive, attacking the matter like a general marshaling an army. Some of us are gentle, allowing the mystery to unfold like a flower.

While there is single right way to engage, there are a fair number of wrong ways. We think we're engaging, when instead we're drifting or full-on marching away from the real matter. This is why a good guide is important. Also important is following whatever way is natural to us, and understanding that our approach will change over the years, even as we do.

Mu is about a truth that is usually hidden from us. The truth is that we are wildly open, boundless, and empty. After first finding our identity with the open, the boundless, the empty, we continue to explore what it means. This can take a while. After living with Mu for a time, we move on to find new koans. Each presents different aspects of reality for exploration and investigation. Each koan becomes a new adventure, a new angle or approach to the matters of our lives.

And the different koan collections offer differing flavors of approach. I want to describe here, just a little, the feel of them.

After unpacking Mu or another koan of fundamental reality, of emptiness, of boundlessness, we take up an in-house miscellaneous koan collection. This collection is often unique to each particular community. In the Boundless Way Community, we adhere to the roughly one hundred questions used in the Diamond Sangha, which are much like those used within the Sanbo Zen community. The White Plum interpolates a list of two hundred here. Sometimes this list is reduced to one hundred. Both are based upon Maezumi Roshi's training with the lay Rinzai master Koryu Osaka Roshi.

With the miscellaneous collections we get a short course in koan presentation and language. Many of these cases are single points from longer and more complicated koans. Some are simple as simple can be. "Stop that distant temple bell," "Go straight on that road with ninety-nine curves," "The true Buddha is sitting in that house." Others push us to our very limits. Which is up to us.

Within the Harada-Yasutani tradition this is followed by two collections that are used in the Takujo Hakuin tradition of orthodox Rinzai. The other possible approach in curricular koan practice is the Inzan Hakuin line. They don't use the books, instead relying on an in-house list. Interestingly, there are also traditional stylistic differences as well.

The Takujo style is generally considered more meticulous, while the Inzan style is more dynamic. And, of course, regardless of the inclination of the various schools, individual teachers bring their own temperament and style. The Inzan curriculum is not represented in any significant way in the West. So back to the books of the Takujo approach.

The first of these books that are explored in depth is the twelfth-century anthology *Wumenguan*, the *Gateless Gate*. It is a bit more rough and ready than the other collections, and I have a deep fondness for it. After that the *Biyan Lu*, the *Blue Cliff Record,* another twelfth-century anthology of one hundred cases. That is, if you count only the cases themselves. If you count all the points, that number more than quadruples.

Those of us who follow the Harada-Yasutani curriculum shift to the traditional Soto collection the *Congrong Lu*, the *Book of Serenity.* Each collection brings additional points of focus. Some are more literary than others. Each text offers its unique angle. We recommend digging in and making this tradition our own.

The Takujo Rinzai curriculum doesn't use the *Book of Serenity*. Instead the next books following the *Blue Cliff Record* are the *Record of Linji (Rinzai)* and the Japanese collection *Entangling Vines*. The Harada-Yasutani collection follows the *Book of Serenity* with the Japanese Soto master Keizan Jokin's *Denkoroku*: *The Record of Transmitting the Lamp*.

Then both the Takujo and Harada-Yasutani return to examine Dongshan Liangjie's *wuwei* or five ranks and the sixteen bodhisattva precepts as koans. In the Takujo line the precepts are examined first and then the five ranks. In the Harada-Yasutani system the five ranks precede the precepts.

All along the way, all along the Way, the practice going forward is very much about bringing realization and daily life together. So perhaps you can really understand what the "oak tree in the garden" means, but can you see it in your spouse who is angry with you in this moment? And how does this inform your actual lived life?

The Zen teacher John Daido Loori observed that moving out of Mu and into the rest of the cases is something like advancing into a new adolescence. Often it is awkward, not fully integrated. Sometimes our manifestation is more childish, while sometimes it is more adult. Each moment is important. And so it is important to not move too quickly, as one engages. We need to allow ourselves to marinate, to integrate, and to see how it manifests in daily life.

## 19

# Three Koans from the Gateless Gate

My favorite anthology of Zen's koans is the *Wumen-guan*, the *Gateless Gate*. It is the first of the traditional books we encounter in the Harada-Yasutani curriculum. And I'm sure that has something to do with my affection for the book. But it is also quite a bit different than the other traditional collections. It is less refined and literary. A bit more up-front and in-your-face.

I find it a perfect source for providing a taste of the koan literature. I include here three cases. The first is actually from the very end of the collection, "Doushuai's Three Barriers," although one encounters it earlier as one of the miscellaneous koans. It touches on life and death. The second case I've chosen is Yunmen's "I Spare You Sixty Blows." It's a great example of that direct pointing, of sincerity in practice, and learning to let go. And, finally, we enter the dream worlds of our spiritual lives with "Yangshan's Sermon from the Third Seat."

## Doushuai's Three Barriers
### GATELESS GATE, CASE 47

The priest Doushuai set up three barriers, three questions for those who walk the Way:

Making your way through the brambles and weeds you give yourself fully to the quest to find your true nature. Right now, dear one, where is your true nature?

Once you realize your true nature, you are free from birth and death. At that last moment as your eyes fall, how are you free from birth and death?

When you are free from birth and death, you will know where to go. So, when the parts that make you all fall apart, where will you go?

Master Doushuai lived at the beginning of the eleventh century. He entered the religious life while still a boy, then after investigating all the major schools of Buddhism available to him at that time, he settled into the Zen Way. He was only forty-eight when he died. But even denied the experiences of old age, the wisdom that comes from experiencing the vagaries of our decline, there's no doubt he touched the whole matter.

While we can be sure of few things, one thing that is relentlessly in our face is mortality, the fact that things end. You and I die. All we know will die. And it doesn't take great analytic powers to notice that cultures themselves end. Even stars die. So we would be foolish indeed to think our lives are some exception. *We. All. Die.*

What I find interesting is that while in the past the destruction of human cultures was always something finite, one culture dies, but another rises; since 1945 we actually have in our hands the power to destroy all human life. In fact, we could take most of the rest of living things along with us.

I'm a child of the atomic age. In my youth I learned to "duck and cover." One of the turning moments in my life came in my adolescence when I noticed the futility of that exercise. I'm sure it has marked me. Maybe similarly to those who live in cultures that believe they're in the end times.

Me, I feel my aches and pains, and it's harder to focus my eyes in the morning. I'm getting old. So, of course, I'm acutely aware of my mortality. All things die. The world is dying. You are dying. As am I.

And with that a question that includes an invitation. Do you want to penetrate to the heart of things before you die? There is a way. And this little koan tells us a bit about how.

It is possible to see this koan's questions as progressive; you start with the quest, you know what to do as you die, you know what to do after you die. Of course, as with so much of the Zen Way, that would be a tad too simple. Or more correctly, too complicated.

I recall one teacher who said if you figure out Mu, the great koan that becomes the first barrier for most who undertake the discipline of koan introspection, she would give you all the rest of the "answers" to the koan curriculum.

What she meant is that when you truly answer one, particularly one like this, you have indeed touched them all. As it turns out, there is always a bit more to do. So answer this one, and I will simply give you another.

But it is a great question. A central question. And the whole of the matter can be resolved, at least in a very important sense, by resolving that first question. You notice there's a problem, you determine to resolve it, and you embark on the Great Way. That means many different ways. In Zen it means learning how to sit. It also means finding a spiritual director. It may mean living in a temple or monastery, for a time or maybe for a lifetime.

But to what purpose? With the first barrier we are given a pointer about the real nature of practice. Dogen's advice to sit down and become Buddha may help clarify the koan point, or the koan point might help clarify Dogen's advice.

Here we are invited into the rising of doubt and the beginning of our quest. From one angle this can be seen as our desire for awakening, our desire to put our hearts at rest. But there's another angle here as well. The universe itself is calling to us. Those very grasses through which we wander, each strand is calling out to us, inviting us into our deepest intimacy.

Possibly, possibly, the whole thing can be found right here. Right at the beginning. Can you see it? Notice it? Feel it? What does that look like?

Then there's that second barrier, our own dying. From one angle it's all pure speculation. Unless, that is, you're dying. And, from another angle, who isn't dying? From that place. From this place? Where is your true nature?

My first book, *This Very Moment*, was published back in 1996. That feels a very long time ago. I explored this koan there. As it turns out it is one of those cases I find draws my heart more clearly than most. In that book I recalled a friend, Bob Jessup. He had recently died from complications of the AIDS virus.

He was a good man, loved by many, certainly by me. His partner, Jim Wilson, told me a small anecdote about those dying days. Jim was sitting with Bob and talking. He was filled with memories and sharing them with his dying partner. Jim said what good times those were. To which Bob replied, "I'm having a good time, now." Just this. Just this. As the breath slips away. Just this.

And finally, the question that traps people a bit more often than the other two, the barrier that people sometimes like to linger at for a while, the one that seems to point to after you're dead? What is that supposed to mean? Heaven? Hell? The next round?

As Bob was at the final stages of his dying people came to visit him. There's something about visiting the dying. It brings out the best or the worst in us. We are confronted with things. Jan and I visited. "We just wanted to say goodbye," she told him. He laughed. "Half of the county wanted to say goodbye."

But some didn't want just to say goodbye. There were other agendas at play. Various messages or advice as to how to do it. Bob would listen politely, and then he asked them not to return. One person was shocked. Okay, a number were unsettled by this response to their blandishments. That person, however, was terribly upset. He said, "You need to process this." Bob looked at him and replied, "I *am* the process."

I am the process. We understand this and all the koans are answered. There is a story of a meeting between the American Unitarian essayist and Transcendentalist Margaret Fuller and the poet Thomas Carlyle. In her style she declared, "I accept the universe." To which the poet is said to have replied, "You had better."

And so—the mushroom cloud has already gathered and dissipated. Now. Death has come and gone. What does that mean to a person of the Way? That is, what does it mean for you? What will you do? What are you going to do?

William Shakespeare sings to the heart of this koan: "So thou shalt feed on death, that feeds on men. And death once dead, there's no more dying then."

## Dongshan's "I Spare You Sixty Blows"
### GATELESS GATE, CASE 15

Dongshan came to see Yunmen. Yunmen asked him, "Where were you most recently?" Dongshan said, "At Chadu." Yunmen said, "Where were you during the summer?" Dongshan said, "At Baozi Monastery in Hunan." Yunmen said, "When did you leave there?" Dongshan said, "August 25." Yunmen said, "I spare you sixty blows." Next day, Dongshan came again and said, "Yesterday you said you spared me sixty blows. I don't know where I was at fault." Yunmen said, "You rice-bag! Do you go about in such a way, now west of the river, now south of the lake?" With this, Dongshan had great satori.

Dongshan Liangjie was one of the great figures in Zen's history and legend. He lived in the ninth century and, with one of his Dharma heirs, is the traditional founder of the Soto school—and with that he is also a direct lineage ancestor of mine. So I reverence him as an ancestor closer to me in many true ways than if by blood. The Dongshan in this case, however, is not the same person. This one, Dongshan Shouchu (who died in about 990), went on to become a master of Linji sect.

And the teacher of his heart would prove to be Yunmen. This is their first meeting. The narrative of the case looks straightforward, at least at the beginning. The old master asks where the younger monk has been, who replies with that account of his meanderings. In fact there's nothing unusual in the account. Traditionally in Chinese Zen monasticism after a period of time, usually about five years, a monk was encouraged to go on pilgrimage. And that's the case for Yunmen at this moment.

So the question is fair. And the response certainly seems to match. But then there's the turn: Yunmen declares, "I spare you sixty blows." Zen is notorious for abrupt and sometimes violent responses. Here the strike of the stick has been rendered symbolically. I spare you a thrashing. Physically, anyway. Of course we all know words can in fact break bones.

Dongshan probably then made his formal bows and withdrew. But that isn't the end of it. He fretted over the encounter.

He probably dropped it into his formal meditation. It's likely that it was his meditation. And the next day he returns to the master and asks a wonderful question. "Why?"

Here we find the heart of the Zen Way. The question. We have many questions in our lives. Where do I come from? Why am I here? Where am I going? And if we take it up as the focus of our spiritual life, we can render it, reduce it, boil it down, and make it present in every moment, holding it and presenting a deep curiosity.

I like thinking of it as a child's questioning. Of course, at some point we might even see the question taking other directions. Who am I? What is this? In the first case of the *Gateless Gate* anthology, we are given the ultimate rendering of the question, a consolidation of all our questions, at least for followers of the Zen Way, of all the questions of the world into one word.

So in this spirit, with this great knot at the heart of our humanity, Dongshan returns to the teacher and puts it all into words the best he can. Words can kill, and they can give life. He takes the universal longing of our human hearts, and really the deep questions of his own life and his own wanderings, and he presents it in the most personal and intimate way possible.

Dongshan asks, "Where have I gone wrong?"

I know that question. I know that phrasing. Perhaps you do as well. Perhaps it can be the expression of your whole life.

And as a reward for opening his heart and showing who he was, Dongshan got a berating. "Rice-bag" is the ultimate insult for a Zen monastic, being described as nothing but a waste of food. Moreover, Dongshan is challenged for doing what he was supposed to do—wandering among the masters, and sitting with his companions of the Way, holding on to nothing, like clouds, like water.

Of course, with that nothing, there was a holding. I certainly know this internal holding, this grasping. I've clung to my wounds, sometimes vastly too long. I've clung to my loves, sometimes much too long. I've held on to some story or another as if for my very life, thinking it can give me meaning.

We can fritter our whole lives away with that grasping, that life-taking clinging to one thing or another, although it usually boils down to a sweet lie we like repeating to ourselves, like Gollum's *Precious*. But Dongshan, he was ripe. He was vulnerable. He brought his question out and it was answered. His hands opened. And he learned a new way of holding.

Five hundred years later Sojun Ikkyu—a fourteenth-century Rinzai monk and poet in Japan—is said to have had his initial awakening while struggling with this fifteenth case in the *Gateless Gate*. I am very fond of his writing. For instance, in Sonya Arutzen's translation:

Every day, priests minutely examine the Law
And endlessly chant complicated sutras.
Before doing that, though, they should learn
How to read the love letters sent by the wind
and rain, the snow and moon.

Ikkyu struggled with this case. At first, if he did it the way
most of us do, by looking at the outside of the question. This
can take a while. And eventually by finding his way into the
inside—where we are all invited on this Way. Ikkyu's own life
was one of wandering with the question. Since being placed
in a temple as young boy, he'd kicked around and studied with
several teachers. Once he felt he found his true teacher in a
master named Ken'o.

With Ken'o he'd begun to truly dig into the matter of just
sitting, zazen, the foundation of all Zen's practices. He became
so close to him that when the master died, after performing the
rites on his behalf, Ikkyu tried to drown himself. Rescued, Ikkyu
resumed his wanderings, until he found the master Kaso, head
of a branch temple of Daitokuji.

This wasn't Ikkyu's first case; he actually seems to have pro-
ceeded through a number before he was given this one. That's
worth noting for those who too tightly connect passing koans
and awakening. I have little doubt Ikkyu's sojourn with each

of them was authentic. But they were intimations of things to come. Echoes from the future of the question asked and answered.

And this particular case must have mirrored his own life in some profound ways, and it worked. I love this case, because it seems to mirror the life of a genuine spiritual pilgrim. We all of us wander, looking for the right practice and the right guides. Me, I danced with Sufis, I sat at the feet of Vedanta monks, I heard Tibetans and Sikhs, Christian priests, and rabbis expound their understanding of the deep currents of their lives. I met many Zen teachers and lingered with several. Perhaps you have done something similar.

Of course the deeper wandering is also there. That wandering within our own hearts—yours and mine—and minds, looking, exploring, lingering, moving on. As that lovely line puts it, we contain multitudes. And we need to become familiar. We need to know the contours. We need to find the intimacy of our questions.

And then a moment comes. For each of us it is something different. For Ikkyu, while deep within the heart of this koan, it was when a band of blind singers came to the temple and performed. The words of the question dropped away, and the whole thing simply presented itself.

Ikkyu saw into the heart of the matter. But even with this deep insight, he had to continue, to deepen more, to understand ever more fully. This is a spiral journey, which we revisit over and over, although never quite in the same way. Stepping from this magical moment he would have other experiences. He would integrate—and he would forget. He would discover anew. And he would, actually, continue to wander in these new ways, with new eyes, with new ears. In that journey, something of a guide for us as well.

But here's a question for you. What distills the questions of your heart? Where is the koan, the matter that needs clarifying for you? Where does the koan, that presentation of reality and invitation into intimacy, bring you?

Rice-bag? Wanderer? Lover of leaving? Do you hear the love letters? They're tumbling from the sky. They're carried by the wind and the rain and the snow and the moon. They're squawked at you by that little band of feral parrots flying by right now.

Why don't you open one and read it? Now might be a good time. . . .

## Yangshan's Sermon from the Third Seat
### GATELESS GATE, CASE 25

Once in a dream the master Yangshan visited Maitreya in the Tushita heaven. He was led to the third seat in the great hall. As he sat, a monk struck the sounding board and announced, "The monk in the third seat will deliver today's sermon."

Yangshan stood, struck the sounding board himself, and said, "The truth of the Great Way is beyond the four propositions and transcends the one hundred negations. Listen. Listen."

Yangshan Huiji was a ninth-century Chan master standing in the fifth generation from Daijian Huineng, a successor to the great Guishan Lingyou. He had studied with several teachers before finding Guishan, and had several awakenings. But it was with Guishan that it all came together.

Guishan was an heir of Baizhang Huaihai and was known for his more gentle way, using symbols and metaphor more than the stick. So when he saw that young Yangshan was ripe, he met him with a gentle pointing. Yangshan asked, "What is the Buddha's true dwelling place?"

Guishan replied, "Consider the great mystery. Turn your attention to that boundless light. At the moment your thoughts about all this are exhausted, you've come to the source. Here you will find true nature is form and emptiness. Here the true Buddha manifests."

There was no stick and no yelling, just words to do the pointing. And for Yangshan, it was the right moment, the time of fulfillment. Or perhaps it was the time of emptying, a time of stepping beyond clinging to form or to emptiness. And with that he found himself standing in the Buddha realm. So in this story a teacher uses image and metaphor to help the student on the Way, by describing the heaven of the Buddha-to-come.

This is a good time to address the concept that living in "this very moment" involves cutting off all thought, that this project somehow has nothing to do with past or future.

In fact, an awakening that has nothing to do with the past or the future is sham. This "awakening" is more like Alzheimer's disease or some similar disorder, where we are robbed of our past and exist only in a constantly shrinking present until finally we forget to breathe. This has nothing to do with Zen.

*Makyo* are those visions that in Zen are sometimes considered "diabolic interference." When a student describes a makyo, a vision or voice or smells out of the ordinary, the Zen teacher's stock response is, "Don't worry, this will pass." And that's more than good advice. It appears people who get stuck in those images, who believe them as some literal revelation, follow a path that does no one any good. (Often it is suggested several religions might be traced to such makyo.)

In my community makyo is respected. Not as the thing in itself, but as something that occurs naturally along the way, when the world we think is the real world is disrupted. These are important moments. Zen teacher Melissa Myozen Blacker warns us, "In Zen practice, we emphasize a delight in paradox and an energetic love of life lived fully."

The Zen teacher Susan Murphy tells a story that captures the possibilities of makyo as dream, as legend, as myth:

There is a strange category of Celtic fairy story, repeated in many forms, in which a young girl takes shelter on a stormy night in a strange house, and the people there have a corpse laid out in the front room. It is the body of a man who has died, and the young girl is granted shelter on condition that she sits up and watches the body all night. She agrees that whatever happens, she will never take her eyes off the body.

So when that man's body suddenly sits up, stares at her, and flies out of the window, she goes with him, clinging on for dear life. He plunges through seas, he thunders across moors, he dives into rivers, he flings himself over mountains, and she never lets go. She has fastened her heart on this unknown business. And at the end of this truly amazing night, they come back to where they began, and she finds that she has, by her absolute fidelity to the task, released him from a spell. He can show her his true face. You could also say she has released herself, when his true face becomes clear to her. It is the face of unconditional love, and nothing is missing anywhere in the world.

Here we find a moment of ripeness. If we're willing, such moments allow us new directions, so listen. Often, awakening experiences are accompanied by makyo, and one needs to be able to sort through these things—yet another reason it is good to have companions and spiritual directors who have walked this way before.

Anyway, in my makyo, there is a scene very much like the Flammarion engraving. But as my head pokes through, what is there is not a bunch of gear-works—but a riot of life. Everything is connected by green shoots, growing, roiling, connecting ants and other animals and rocks and dirt and planets and stars— and let's not forget about you and me. Each is rising out of the great web of a mother tree's roots and tendrils, existing for its time, and then falling back to the tree.

Regarding these experiences, I inwardly offered myself the advice I would to a student: listen and watch, but don't cling; don't follow in some abstruse analysis. These words and images that rise in the mind may represent the world in the ways that allow us to walk and engage. After all, our minds work metaphorically, and words and emotions are actually not different things. The image arises.

Notice it; no need to follow it.

Just let it be.

## 20

# The Five Ranks

THERE ARE VARIOUS MAPS of the spiritual path. On the Zen Way the most famous are the ten oxherding pictures. And there are many others. However, I suggest digging into just five can be enough to give us a sense of how this dynamic happens, and how we can grow deeper. Dongshan Liangjie, a ninth-century Chinese master and one of the founders of the Soto lineage, adapted five images out of the *I Ching*, the ancient Taoist Book of Change, to guide us into a deeper understanding of this dynamic quality of reality.

They are the five ranks, or sometimes the five modes, possibly a bit more accurately. They have become the final koan of the Rinzai school and the penultimate koan collection within the Harada-Yasutani curriculum. Here we dig ever more fully into the matters of form and emptiness. We are confronted with the relationship between the "relative" or "apparent" or "phenomenal," and the "absolute" or "real" or "empty." And it is here we begin to see the movement of our experience as we come to spiritual maturity.

In the translations handed down in Robert Aitken's lineage, the first verse is titled "Arriving within the Empty."

> In the third watch of the night
> Before the moon appears,
> No wonder when we meet
> There is no recognition!
> Still cherished in my heart
> Is the beauty of earlier days.

Here we are in absolute darkness. This is the samadhi of complete emptiness. All thoughts have fallen away. There is only the moonless dark. This is the awakening we usually call *kensho*. It happens the moment we break through the apparent barrier of our skin and discover we truly are something vast and large. Here, at this moment, everything falls apart.

We understand the mystery of, for instance, the words of Jesus. How the birds of the air have their nests, and the animals of the field their burrows—but the child of humanity has no place to rest her head. There is a similar Zen saying about not having a clot of earth upon which to stand.

There is no room for something else, no space in the universe for a second thing. We see how all things and we ourselves are in truth empty. Seeing this is a powerful experience, one that can be truly liberating. Often people who've walked the Way come to this experience and feel they've accomplished the goal. No doubt it is a profound accomplishment—but as Shitou's famous Zen poem says, "To encounter the absolute is not yet enlightenment."

When people "answer" their first koan, they're demonstrating this understanding. In the Harada-Yasutani schools, this is seen as so important that, for years and years, it was the norm that when one had this breakthrough during a Zen retreat, there would be a celebration and a formal public acknowledgment ceremony.

While we no longer do that ceremony in the lineages within which I've practiced, the significance of this experience is still truly very near the heart of what we are about. Here all our energy, all our effort, everything that we've poured into our practice opens us to something—to *this*. We come to our own deeply personal experience of the empty. Silence. Our own sense of who we are perhaps becomes unclear. We experience the real, but there is nothing to say, nothing to think. Silence. Here we rest, where we know the world of experience is nothing other than the Great Emptiness.

And the shadow of this experience is to sit too comfortably within emptiness. This is the trap of nondifferentiation. Here there is no concern. There is no self and other. This place of emptiness is vast, and it is easy to stay, or at least easy to *want* to stay. The temptation can be very strong to stay in this place of no place. This is what Wumen calls "the dead person breathing."

But in fact we don't stay there. There is that small seed, perhaps not even noticed, like the eye in each of the tadpoles of the yin yang symbol, the tai chi, the grand ultimate. It becomes a stirring in the sleep and the silence. Reality really is dynamic. And within the five ranks there is motion, and within the traditional ordering, next we find our "arriving within phenomena."

> A sleepy-eyed grandma
> Encounters herself in an old mirror.
> Clearly she sees a face,
> But it doesn't resemble hers at all.
> Too bad, with a muddled head,
> She tries to recognize her reflection.

Here consciousness re-emerges. Coming out of the dark, we see ourselves anew. We gaze upon our original face. Where could we ever have thought we would go? A moment before we were on the great path, but now where are we? We discover the singing and dancing that is our true heritage; it is the true Buddha Way.

The traditional image for this experience is of an old woman seeing herself reflected in an ancient mirror. We move from the darkness into the light, from the empty and out into the phenomenal universe. We see our own image, and we know it really is empty. It is our original face from before our parents were born. Here most ideas of self and other vanish, and we know who we are. You know who you are. I know who I am.

Here there is the movement of compassion. We see ourselves in each other, and we know that our actions are all informed by the great emptiness, by radical openness. The shadow here is a lack of moral perspective. Everything is precious, regardless— and so good and evil collapse into each other; there are no decisions, and consequences don't matter.

Still, there is motion. The empty and the phenomenal each take their place in turn. Our consciousness dances from the vast emptiness to the realm of form, spinning throughout the ages of our lives. The basic dynamic is this movement from our experience of the one to our experience of our ordinary lives, where there is high and low, good and ill, and our actions all have consequences.

But there is another motion possible. Next we come to a place experienced as the grand synthesis of self and other. Here we find "phenomena within the empty":

> Within nothingness there is a path
> Leading away from the dusts of the world.
> Even if you observe the taboo

On the present emperor's name,
You will surpass that eloquent one of yore
Who silenced every tongue.

Here we discover a mind as vast as the cosmos. There are no names; the emperor or the world itself cannot be trapped in such a mundane way. Acting from this perspective you have the same mind as the Buddha. And from here we find ourselves moving from the vast silence *toward* something.

Our actions are completely informed by our certain knowledge of our true nature. In the Rinzai tradition this is where we live the enlightened life, where our actions are informed by our deepest knowing of who we are. We find our true freedom in our actual actions. One has grown up, become a spiritual adult.

In this moment we experience wisdom, our knowing of how we are the same and how we are different. Still, a shadow can appear. We forget the suffering of humanity in the face of its beauty. We can get lost in a realm a little too pure, a little too far above the fray. This is what's called "the stink of Zen." Remember, fish cannot live for very long in pure water.

Fortunately there still is motion. The fourth rank is the "empty within phenomena":

When two blades cross points,
There's no need to withdraw.

The master swordsman
Is like the lotus blooming in the fire.
Such a man has in and of himself
A heaven-soaring spirit.

Here our understanding and our actions are both informed from the depths. Don't be misled by the image of two blades. This points to the full expression of our understanding, both emptiness and our ordinary lives: sharp, present, luminous. The lotus is the central image, a flower blooming in the midst of fire: the enlightened life lived within the world. Just this. The smallest action is the work of the Buddha. To sweep the floor, to clean a toilet, to play with a child; in these actions, the buddha realms are revealed, heaven is opened to us all.

Here one becomes wise. Even the least well read, even the most sheltered life becomes informed; the simplest words express the Great Way. We have a sense of balance and harmony, and we understand when to act and when to refrain from acting.

Everything is perceived within its uniqueness: alone, beautiful, never to be repeated. Here we really understand our neighbor as our very self—and here compassion manifests in every action, every word.

We begin to free ourselves of shadows. We know the other as our very self. But that in itself can be a shadow, a forgetting of the dark in the blazing beauty of being. Still, there is saving motion, keeping us from the stultification of purity.

And here we come finally to the fifth rank, the "arrival within both at once":

> Who dares to equal the one
> Who falls into neither being nor non-being!
> All men want to leave
> The current of ordinary life,
> But he, after all, comes back
> To sit among the coals and ashes.

One teacher describes this as the moment the river flows into the ocean. As we walk along the shore, the waves wash up, and there is no trace in the sand. Our very ordinariness is enlightenment. Our thoughts, our actions, each thing of us, is the blessed land, is the action of the Buddha.

While we are active in the world, we do not lose our understanding of the empty. Here our struggle is over—yet still we care. If those we are with are sad, so are we. If our companions are happy, so are we. We sit by the dying fire, and even the word *Zen* is forgotten at this moment.

The verse speaks of this moment as one where we fall into neither "yes" nor "no." Others may strive, but at this moment the true student of the Way unites everything. She sits quietly by the fire; he sits languidly astride the lion. Here the phenomenal and the empty so completely interpenetrate that there is no consciousness of either. The ancients speak of this moment as when self and other, every thread of a thought of self and other, completely fall away.

Here our shadows and the light are one thing—and we move gracefully in the world. Our actions are pure; our refraining from actions is pure. Now, there are two points that need to be upheld here. First, this "purity" does not mean we somehow no longer can cause harm. And, second, all of this arises completely within the natural world, within the play of cause and effect. Here we encounter the upright Way, one of full responsibility, one where we are completely intimate with ourselves, with each other, with that radical openness.

But it is graceful, and ordinary. It is the place of that tenth image in another Zen map of the human condition, the ten oxherding pictures, where a fat man enters the village with a bag of gifts slung over his shoulder. In one version this picture is titled "Returning to the World with Bliss-Bestowing Hands."

HOPEFULLY a reflection on these five ranks gives us some sense of the exact identity of the phenomenal universe with our very selves and the emptiness that is shunyata. Also, and most important, I hope this brief description evinces the dynamic quality of these aspects of reality. I hope this shows how they differentiate and inform each other, and how each perspective brings strengths and, to some degree, weaknesses.

The true Way is one of being ordinary, where we have shortcomings and gifts. But as we engage it fully, it all becomes a blessing.

And I hope it speaks to the nature of wisdom on this Way that is Zen Buddhism. This Zen Way we are walking has nothing to do with retreat from the world. Rather it is about our most intimate connection with the world wherever we find ourselves, meditating in a monastery, washing dishes in our home, or doing business on Wall Street.

Now, one more caution is important here. It would be a mistake to take the apparent teleology, the seeming direction of these five ranks, as more than utilitarian. Again, the real world is dynamic, and the intricacies of relationship are so vast one can never say with certainty what a "direction" might or should be. We can experience all these spiritual states at different times without any specific progression.

So don't fall into the trap that even these words of mine can set for you. Don't get tangled in the web. Don't mistake my pointing finger for your experience. Rather, just open yourself to the possibility of actual experience, of actual intimacy. If we do this, if you do this, here you can find another tangling.

Recall that line from our ancestor Wumen commenting on the koan Mu, and know that at the moment of your own realization of deepest intimacy, of knowing your identity with shunyata, you will "walk hand in hand with the whole descending line of patriarchs and be eyebrow to eyebrow with them. You will see with the same eye that they see with, hear with the same ear that they hear with."

# 21

# The Buddhist Precepts as Koans

CONTRARY to the solipsistic misunderstanding of Zen Buddhism promulgated here and there, particularly on the web, Zen is not a spiritual anarchist's fantasy. When we begin to investigate ourselves and our place in the world, one of the first things we find is that we do not exist in isolation. It's not all about me, and it's not all about you—never has been. And we invite terrible consequences when we fail to understand this.

Here is an inescapable truth: everything we do has consequences. So we need some external guidelines, some trustworthy set of rules by which to measure what we're doing.

Frankly, there are times when we just need rules—for much of our lives we're wandering around in the thickets. We haven't a clue. We're lost. And the Buddhists precepts can become a lifeline thrown out to us. And sometimes we just have to grab that line; sometimes we just have to follow the rules.

At the same time, if we live only in the realm of rules, we are strangled by dead letters. Not only are our lives constrained, we become caricatures of our true potentiality. We need to recall how we are profoundly tied up together, how our individual lives, our very intimate personal existence, are completely woven out of each other.

It's not all about me, not all about you—and also, it is. We are more intimate than the words can ever convey. We are all relatives, all family. And there are ways to encounter the words, "do not kill, do not steal, do not lie, do not misuse your sexuality, and do not become intoxicated," and so on, that become the living expressions of this intimate dance of life. The precepts open to a way of life that is creative, expressive, and inviting.

In each moment of our lives—as we open our mouths to speak, as we encounter each "other" in our lives, as we seek intimate moments with another, as we face death—our practice is to try to be present, to be clear.

As we undertake the Middle Way, and specifically the path of Zen, we undertake much more than a meditation discipline. There is that great insight into form and emptiness, and there is a path of manifestation in our daily lives. This takes form in Japanese-derived Soto Zen as the sixteen bodhisattva precepts. They begin with the three refuges, include the three pure precepts, and conclude with the ten grave precepts.

We can engage the precepts in a wide number of ways. At the

beginning, and also along the Way, they can just be the rules. These rules can be a protection of self and other—and they can also become a stick to beat self or other. We need to be careful. When do we follow these rules? When do we break them?

But each and every one of them is also an invitation into the fundamental matter. In the realm of absolute emptiness, where is "not killing," where is "not stealing"? What can be killed? What can be stolen? Even these powerful rules burn away like mist in the morning sun—but I hope it is obvious we cannot simply rest there. As we are open, receptive, not judging, as we allow these things to appear and disappear, a compassionate perspective arises within us. Without compassion, the Zen Way has no power at all.

From that perspective we can examine the particular. How does this specific precept serve human beings and the world in this specific moment? How does it relate to the rest of those precepts in this specific moment? What fosters generosity and care? What points us beyond the rules in a way that does not ignore them?

All of this is dynamic.

Particularly at the beginning, we take refuge within the Way as we would take refuge from a storm—realizing how important it is to acknowledge we need help. And this is foundational to everything else we do on the Zen Way.

Aitken Roshi said the three refuges are much like the Christian communion. I wondered about that the first time I heard it, but gradually I've realized he put his finger right on the point. It is a moment where we take something totally ordinary, and by giving it our attention and our confidence, something weirdly wonderful happens.

On the Buddhist Way there are three facets to this way of refuge: the Buddha, the Dharma, and the Sangha.

Here *Buddha* principally means the Buddha of history, Gautama Siddhartha—that distant figure obscured and magnified by the mists of time. And certainly he is the originator of our feast. Without a doubt, this is Buddha.

But *Buddha* means "awake," and refers also to all those teachers of awakening, including everyone who touched our heart and pointed us in a healthful direction. In my case, I think of Jesus and Mohammed and the little girl who walked up to me in Target and asked me to tie her shoe. Buddha is all these.

In our times some of us speak of "higher power." In the twelve-step traditions, I think this points, in part, to the reality that we don't do it on our own. Actually, I believe they say we can't do it on our own. We each have to find what that means for ourselves. But this mysterious stretching beyond our own egos, our own sense of what we can and what we cannot do, is so important. So Buddha is this as well.

*Buddha* is past all personalities and becomes the face of emptiness itself. So Buddha is also the great not-knowing.

And taking refuge in Buddha is taking refuge in all of this.

*Dharma* is an even more complicated and elusive term than *Buddha*. It has no obvious comparable word in English. The Sanskrit root means "to hold," or "to maintain," or "to keep." And from that it is often translated as "law" or "doctrine." *Dharma* is also a term for the constituent elements of reality, usually written in English with a lowercase *d* to distinguish it from the more spiritual significance. *Dharma* has become a technical term in all the religions of the Indian subcontinent.

In Buddhism, Dharma tends to mean both the teachings of the Buddha himself and, by extension, all Buddhist teachings. So Dharma includes the four noble truths and the eightfold path—and all the rest. It also is understood as "ultimate truth." One commentator suggests it is similar to the Christian theological term *logos*, with its connotations of "word" and "reason."

For us on the Zen Way, Dharma is additionally enriched by the fact that it is translated as *Dao* in China. Many of the Chinese Daoist senses of the word were added, including "absolute principle," the metaphysics of yin and yang, and harmony with nature.

*Sangha* was first used as a term for the monastic community of the Buddha's followers. Specifically it meant a gathering of four or more ordained individuals, and in some schools of Buddhism that remains the definition. But in the Mahayana, *Sangha* is often much more broadly understood. It refers to the great community of Buddha's followers, like the word *church* in Christianity.

But in Zen particularly this community is vastly larger yet. It includes mammals and reptiles; it includes birds, and insects, and fish, and mushrooms. It includes the air and rocks and the ocean. It includes planets, and stars, and galaxies, and black holes. All of this is Sangha.

And, so, that refuge in the storm that is Buddha and Dharma and Sangha is the foundation. All else follows.

The three pure precepts are a summation statement. They derive from a *gatha* or saying attributed to the Buddha. In the Dhammapada collection, one version is:

> Cease from all evil;
> Practice all good,
> Keep your mind pure—
> Thus all the Buddhas taught.

Gradually the lines morphed. As Aitken Roshi observed, "In Mahayana Buddhism, these lines underwent a change reflecting a shift from the ideal of personal perfection to the ideal of oneness with all beings." So in the Zen precepts, the third line is modified to reflect that larger view, and the last dropped.

> Cease from all evil;
> Practice all good;
> Save the many beings.

From there, we move to the ten grave precepts. The first five are basically the five precepts the Buddha gave to everyone. The others are adapted from the Brahmajala Sutra. There are a handful of books that address these precepts, or most of them, from a Zen perspective. I particularly recommend Robert Aitken's foundational *The Mind of Clover*, Reb Anderson's *Being Upright*, Diane Rizzetto's *Waking Up to What You Do*, Daido Loori's *The Heart of Being*, and finally the latter part of my own *If You're Lucky, Your Heart Will Break*, which is largely concerned with the precepts as well.

The ten grave precepts presented as vow are:

1. Recognizing I am not separate from all that is, I vow to take up the Way of Not Killing.
2. Being satisfied with what I have, I vow to take up the Way of Not Stealing.
3. Honoring mutuality and respecting commitment, I vow to take up the Way of Not Misusing Sex.

4. Listening and speaking from the heart, I vow to take up the Way of Not Speaking Falsely.

5. Cultivating a mind that sees clearly, I vow to take up the Way of Not Intoxicating Mind and Body.

6. Unconditionally accepting what each moment has to offer, I vow to take up the Way of Not Finding Faults with Others.

7. Meeting others on equal ground, I vow to take up the Way of Not Elevating Myself at the Expense of Others.

8. Using all the ingredients of my life, I vow to take up the Way of Not Sparing the Dharma Assets.

9. Transforming suffering into wisdom, I vow to take up the Way of Not Harboring Ill Will.

10. Honoring my life as an instrument of the Great Way, I vow to take up the Way of Not Defaming the Three Treasures.

For now, let's go over just a few briefest of pointers for each of these precepts.

FIRST IS THAT mystery of life, the precept of not killing. It is actually a conundrum of the first order. As written, there appears to be no exceptions—just no killing, of anything ever.

And so with every breath there is some violation, with every step some breaking of this precept.

On the other hand, this is often understood as cherishing and encouraging life. I find it an invitation into the kinship of all things, a reminder that even our food is a relative, and we cannot live without the sacrifice of many others.

Daido Loori tells an anecdote about driving at night and hitting a raccoon. He stopped the car, got out, and saw the animal was dying. The merciful thing would have been to back the car over the raccoon and end the suffering. Instead, for all the complicated reasons of our humanity, he got back in his car and drove off. That act haunted him for years after.

As he notes in his book, "My own self-centeredness, squeamishness, and fear prevented me from taking its life and putting it out of its misery." To the point, he adds, "I violated the precept 'do not kill,' because I did not have the heart to kill that raccoon. My own feelings were more important than the agony of that creature."

So, here, I hope we see we're not being invited into some simple set of rules, but rather we're being invited into the most complex of relationships, with reality itself, in all its messiness, within all its possibilities for good and for ill.

The second precept is an invitation to understanding the very shape of the world: not stealing. Here we find ourselves constantly called to the reality of differentiation, and that our lives are constant negotiations with limitations. Finding boundaries and knowing when to break them is the constant challenge of living.

Aitken Roshi was pretty sure that property itself is theft. "Property is theft" is a line coined by a French anarchist in the nineteenth century. It is something of a hallmark of Marxism if not socialism in general. I think property can indeed be theft, but I don't agree in any general universal way. I don't find it a moral injunction.

So I find myself disagreeing about something pretty fundamental with one of my most important teachers. Which leaves me with two points to consider. The first raises the nature of my relationship with my teachers and mentors. When do I bow, and when do I disagree? The second forces me to consider what exactly is theft. How do I understand it? Through the light of my Dharma practice, and my life, how do I understand theft?

In her study of the precepts, the Zen teacher Diane Rizzetto opens the chapter on not stealing with a comment from Henry Miller: "Giving and receiving are at bottom one thing, dependent upon whether one lives open or closed. Living openly one becomes a medium, a transmitter; living thus, as a river, one experiences life to the full, flows along with the current of life, and dies in order to live again as an ocean." I find this a powerful pointer.

Next is the precept about our being bodies: not misusing sexuality. The original form of this precept was simply to refrain from all sexual activity. A second-best approach was sexual expression solely within the bounds of marriage. The realities of the complexities of our sexuality have been part of modernity— and so for a contemporary student of the Way, fully engaging this powerful part of our lives is immensely important. With an honest engagement, we find ourselves called to see ourselves as sexual beings and to find ways of expression that are healthy and supportive of our human condition.

Diane Rizzetto calls this taking up "the way of engaging in sexual intimacy respectfully and with an open heart." Here there is no doubt we're walking dangerous ground. As she observes, "If there is anything that can broadside our thoughts and emotions, it's sexual desire." I look into my own heart. I consider the feelings that rise in my body, so animal, so primitive, so compelling—and I stand in awe of the mystery. I find myself painfully aware of how much lives just below the bubbles of my conscious life.

Here we are at our most animal; and it can be frightening. But also it is where we are most alive, and so finding our way through this tangle of heart and body is something as important as breathing. And finding our way as sexual beings is fully the heart of our way as spiritual beings.

Then there is the wondrous beauty of words, the precept of not lying. Again, within the great empty, we manifest in a thousand million ways. We are invited to recall that words themselves do matter. They can both kill and give life.

The Korean teacher Seung Sahn liked to posit situations where keeping one precept would force us to break another. You find yourself sitting on a log, for example, in a glade in the wilderness. Suddenly a fox appears out of the woods and dashes under the log. Within scant minutes a hunter appears and asks, "Where is the fox?" The old teacher liked to make sure you were forced here to speak. No noble silence permitted (the hunter aims the gun at you), so speaking truthfully kills the fox, not speaking kills you. An obvious answer would be to say, "It went that way," and point on to the other side of the glade.

What do we do? Sometimes we have to speak. Sometimes the straight-ahead truth does not seem right or good. What then? What now?

Then there is the admonition to remain clear, and the precept of no intoxicants. How we cloud our mind is a constant revelation. Drugs. Alcohol. Television. Daydreams. When are they appropriate? When are they not?

This might seem pretty easy. However, the Zen teacher Reb

Anderson notes, "If you feel an impulse to turn away, to modify your sacred being, refraining or restraining are no longer possible, because the impulse has already happened." The trap began with the first longing even before it turned into a thought.

From here, we start slicing and dicing our behaviors even more carefully, with the call to skillful presence, the precept of not speaking of others' faults. Here we find the call into community, to being present to each other, and to celebrate when we can. It is also a push to not set ourselves up as judge, jury, and, on occasion, executioner. And with that, the challenge is to live authentically, and generously.

It is not easy. As the spiritual leader in his community, Aitken Roshi wrote:

When I hear people condemn a fellow student in our sangha, I acknowledge my own faults, my own inadequacy as a teacher, for my students have not yet touched the place where there are no faults, and are not, in the instance at hand, practicing to reach that place.

When is that place? Where is that place?
And I find that leads directly into the way of the small, the precept of not praising one's self at the expense of others. With this we find one more invitation into that generosity which is

both the heart of and the fulfillment of our path. There are some harsh self-assessments to be made. Can we only find validation by demeaning others? What does the world look like when our sense of self is found in complementing others instead of recounting the losses of others?

Rizzetto writes:

> During the Vietnam war, the Vietnamese Zen teacher Thich Nhat Hanh spoke before a liberal, politically active audience in Berkeley, California. When asked about taking political action, he told the audience that taking action was important, but more important was to try to remember that they are not helping bring peace as long as they place themselves in a morally superior position.

It is hard. It can be much harder than we might think, until we start noticing how we interact with others.

The next precept has to do with not being greedy. Generosity—with our words, with our actions, with our attention—is clearly a hallmark of the Way.

There's a story I've always liked about a man who goes to the priest after the Sunday service and says, "I'm sorry, I made a mistake. I meant to put a dollar bill into the collection plate, but I accidentally put in a hundred-dollar bill. I'd like it back."

To which the priest replies, "Well, no. You gave that to God, and now it belongs to the divine."

After a bit of back and forth, the man saw he was not going to get the hundred-dollar bill back. So in surrender he said, "At least I'll have a hundred dollars banked in heaven."

To which the priest replied, "No, actually you have one dollar banked in heaven."

How we engage, how we give, matters. The generous heart, whether with money or with the teachings themselves (the precept's original meaning), matters for everything.

The next precept, the precept of not being hateful, takes us directly to Guanyin's thousand hands. While this precept is sometimes called "not indulging in anger," there is in fact nothing inherently wrong with the arising anger. Anger can be the most appropriate response to a particular situation. Sometimes it is a visceral pressing call, to fix something. But when we foster anger, it festers, and it becomes a cancer on our hearts. Hate is that clinging anger. Facing it, dealing with it, we find something larger, something more useful.

So we're invited to investigate our hearts, and watch our reactions. In Dianne Rizzetto's book, she quotes one of her students, "Anger no longer seems a lunatic stranger locked in the basement, but a familiar shadowy twin who suddenly appears in the room in unexpected guises."

And last we're called into loving the Way, with the precept of "not disparaging the three treasures." The Way itself is constantly presenting. If we do not turn from it, we can open possibilities for ourselves and for others. Something past important, and something always waiting, for as long as our hearts beat, for as long as we take a breath.

As Daido Loori tells us, "Precepts are Buddha, Buddha is precepts. Each time we acknowledge that we have drifted off a precept, take responsibility and return to the precept, we are manifesting the wisdom and compassion of the Tathagata."

Things, actions, and thoughts are themselves expressions of the manifold reality in which we live. They are gates into the great empty, inviting us into compassionate expression. We are invited into exploring the nature of all things as we examine them in their literal ways. As we open ourselves to seeing they are completely empty, completely vacant, they point to the great dynamic—the dance of perspective—and they are compassion itself.

In short, they are the Way.

# PART THREE

# Living Zen

## 22

# Five Styles of Zen

As it matured, Zen proved to be dynamic. From the beginning its insights and disciplines appealed to both Buddhists and non-Buddhists. Guifeng Zongmi, who taught in the late eighth and early ninth centuries, outlined what he saw as the principal ways of engaging Zen. He was considered a great scholar as well as a teacher of considerable merit. We in the Zen schools share him with the Huayan, or Flower Ornament, School, which also considers him an ancestor. Somehow that broadness feels particularly appropriate in someone who explored the breadth as well as the depth of Zen.

Guifeng was concerned with the polemics between advocates of sudden awakening and gradual cultivation within Zen. He offered a subtle and important corrective, pointing out there were in fact five styles of Zen. I find them very helpful. Anyone embarking on an exploration of Zen in the West today will find all five versions being taught somewhere by someone. (In fact, his thesis was reworked by Haku'un Yasutani Roshi in *The Three Pillars of Zen*, which remains an important classic.)

Guifeng's first style is *bompu* Zen, or "ordinary Zen." I think another good term for this approach is "secular Zen." This is Zen taken on for personal well-being, for our physical or mental health. Many people come to Zen because they heard they could lower their blood pressure through meditation. In our contemporary Western culture, many people practice Mindfulness-Based Stress Reduction. Developed by Jon Kabat-Zinn and his associates, MBSR could be seen as a sort of *bompu* Buddhist practice.

There is nothing wrong with this approach. Many people who start Zen for health reasons eventually shift to more traditionally spiritual motivations. A drawback to this list is that it's tempting to rank these five styles hierarchically from the "worst" (dualistic Zen) to the "best" (perfected Zen). In fact, each of these can ultimately function as a gate to Zen in all its depth.

However, like any human creation, each of these gates has its own shadows. Yasutani's critique of bompu Zen is that within it one will likely remain stuck in the fundamentally dualistic mind. Practicing to improve one's problems can leave us in our confused state. Being content with merely fixing things falls well short of what Zen is in fact offering.

The second of the categories of Zen is *gedo*, or "outside the Way." It is the adaptation of Zen within religious or spiritual but still non-Buddhist contexts. Example are the practices of Zen taken up by Christians, including clergy. Personally, I admire much of what I'd call "Christian Zen." Christian Zen teacher Ruben Habito's wonderful and inviting book *Living Zen, Loving God,* for instance, shows that this is an authentic, powerful, and beautiful path.

My observation of this embrace of Zen by practitioners of other traditions is generally positive. It can help them deepen their own spiritual path. Zen's disciplines become a sort of supercharger, injecting the power of presence into pretty much any tradition's spiritual practices. "Flow," as presented by modern psychologist Mihaly Csikszentmihalyi in his book with that title, is one contemporary manifestation of gedo Zen.

Yasutani Roshi warns of one less valuable version of gedo Zen, practiced by those who cultivate supernatural powers. This practice particularly builds up *joriki*, the power of a focused mind. Because it has such seductive, appealing power, it can cause people to miss out on the deeper gifts of Zen.

The third is *shojo* Zen, which focuses on the advantages to the self. Traditionally it is pejoratively called Hinayana (small vehicle) Zen. This entangles us in polemics between the two great schools of Buddhism, the Mahayana (the self-declared "greater" vehicle) and the Theravada (self-described "school of the elders"). Mahayanists demean the school of the elders by calling it the "small vehicle."

Rejecting the idea that the Theravada is a lesser vehicle, we also need to let go of the laden term *Hinayana*. Recognizing that the shojo style of Zen is unrelated to the historic distinctions between schools of Buddhism, we can consider Guifeng's real point. There is a style of meditation that is a "smaller" way. Shojo is a self-centered and selfish approach to the disciplines, concerned exclusively with one's own state. Again, it is a form of dualism, more subtle than seeking a healthy body or mind, and therefore harder to correct. This is contrasted with the view of the Mahayana, framing practice as not only for ourselves but for all beings.

Next is *godo* Zen, or "Buddhist Zen." This is the Zen of awakening. It is found in the rising of the bodhi mind—that desire to awaken to what is. It's true that this desire is, after all, a desire, a form of the "gaining mind" dream. But this is also often a gate as well. Handled properly it becomes bodhi mind, the mind of nondual awakening—and within that movement is the godo approach.

Godo Zen is also very much the Zen of koan introspection. Godo opens our deepest insight into what zazen is. As Yasutani Roshi writes, echoing Dogen Zenji, "The more deeply you experience *satori* (enlightenment, awakening), the more deeply you perceive the needs for practice." This is the manifestation of what is sometimes called "practice/realization." It is the very heart of shikantaza, just sitting.

Finally, there's *saijojo* Zen, "perfected Zen," where striving and realization itself are found to be one. This is the Zen of Shakyamuni Buddha—and of all the buddhas of past, present, and future. It is the Zen of "returning to the world with bliss-bestowing hands." All we do and everything we are becomes the simple manifestation of awakening.

Saijojo Zen is also the way of pure shikantaza. Its danger is the seduction of just sitting without awakening, where the actual leap beyond self and other remains an idea rather than one's life.

Yasutani Roshi states that these last two forms of Zen are complementary. Properly engaged, they present two avenues to the same place, where the way of *kensho* (seeing through the self) and koan introspection leads to the subtle wisdom of just sitting—where just sitting becomes the koan "sit down and become Buddha," which can fully awaken the heart-mind.

## 23

# Zen and Western Culture

ZEN COMING WEST has had several powerful and transformative encounters. The meetings with Christianity and Judaism
have been significant. Even more, the encounter with the scien-
tific worldview has been disruptive, challenging, and, I believe,
fruitful. A principal subset of this encounter has been the meeting of Zen and Western psychology.

Another wildly transformative engagement has been that
of Zen with the feminism and gender equality in the West.
This has been rich and difficult. The self-examination this has
demanded of practitioners has been powerful, and the rise of
women in leadership has no parallel in the history of Buddhism.

Today, nearly half of all Zen teachers in the West are women,
including some of the most prominent. I think of Jan Chozen
Bays, Melissa Myozen Blacker, Joan Halifax, Zenkei Blanche
Hartman, Wendy Egyoku Nakao, Pat Enkyo O'Hara, Barbara
Rhodes, and Joan Sutherland—and this is just the start to a

significantly long list. A powerful, compelling presentation of the reality that women have been an integral part of the Buddhadharma from its inception and especially within Zen is Florence Caplow and Susan Moon's *The Hidden Lamp: Stories from Twenty-Five Centuries of Awakened Women.*

GLBTQ practitioners have simply become part of the Western Buddhist world. Issan Dorsey, the Soto Zen priest and founding abbot of the Hartford Street Zen Center in San Francisco, was among the first openly GLBTQ practitioners. Dorsey Roshi was instrumental in the formation of the Maitri Hospice and later the renowned Zen Hospice Project.

Teachers of color are finding their way as significant contributors to our formation as a Western Zen. One of the great wounds of our Western Zen is found in the divide between those who are the children of the Asian diaspora and the convert community. As an example we see two organizations supporting the emergence of Soto Zen here in North America. The one, the Soto Zen Buddhist Association, consists largely of convert Buddhists, while the other, the Association of Soto Zen Buddhists, is predominantly Japanese or of Japanese descent. Some of this is institutional, as there are substantial differences in training expectations between the two groups. But there are other aspects that hang uncomfortably in the air.

And things are changing. Here in the West where the convert

community consists largely of people of European descent, we now include American teachers with Asian roots like Jakusho Kwong and Wendy Egyoku Nakao; Latinx teachers such as James Cordova and Daniel Terragno; and teachers of African descent such as Merle Kodo Boyd, Jules Shuzen Harris, Zenju Earthlyn Manuel, and angel Kyodo williams.

Each of these encounters is mutually transformative. I find the possibilities for Zen forming in the West rich and breathtaking, constantly challenging our ideas of status quo, constantly enlarging our vision. But that's the deal: we engage, we open our hearts, we put our minds to work, and things happen.

## 24

# Zen Training and Zen Teachers for the West

I'VE MET MANY PEOPLE who attend a period of Zen meditation and exclaim how wonderful it was. And then they declare they will sit two hours a day for the rest of their lives. Experience has taught me that this will be likely their last visit to our Zen group.

I believe that what it takes to become an authentic Zen practitioner is pretty simple. One needs a regular meditation practice. I believe the bare minimum is about half an hour a day, most every day. Yes, more is arguably better. But that minimum is sufficient to shift our lives. If you can devote that much time to the project, you're doing Zen practice.

I also want to say you don't have to start there. At the very beginning regularity is more important than duration. So ten minutes, even five minutes, three times a week starts you on your way. Then build up the practice until you can do that half an hour. If your life allows a half an hour in the morning and another in the evening, even better.

It helps to join a Zen group. The majority of Zen groups in this country meet only once a week. Be a little careful about the group. Learn something about its members. Google can be very, very helpful. The sangha doesn't have to be perfect. It just has to be constant, and the leaders have to be devoted to serving the Dharma rather than their own egos or pocketbooks. Then let that group become the anchor for your practice.

That's the basics of what it takes to be a Zen practitioner. But there is more on offer. If you possibly can, attend retreats. One day, three days, five days, and seven days are common numbers for Zen-style retreats. Sometimes, for some people, this just isn't possible. And, again, you can get what you need with a simply daily practice. But the value of the retreat practice cannot be overemphasized.

And, last, it is wise to have a guide on the way of awakening. No tradition owns awakening. The great insights of intimacy are open to all human beings and found in every tradition, and outside tradition.

That said, there are ways that increase our odds of experiencing the great opening of heart and mind. Zen, in my opinion, is among the clearest of these possible ways. It offers the practices that are the primary subject of this little book. I find them the most profitable of the many spiritual technologies human beings have devised. Zen also offers guides on the Way.

It is important for someone on the Zen Way to find spiritual direction. At the very least we need a coach for our practice. But, really, to go to the depths we need more. We need someone who will hold up the mirror, who will offer corrections, and who will point and sometimes push us in the right direction. On this Way a teacher is not just important but critical.

So who are these teachers? And how do we know if they're competent? How can we sort for wheat and chaff among those who present themselves as guides and counselors? It is not always obvious, and titles alone are not sufficient. But there are some characteristics common among Zen teachers, and we can look for those.

Within the various training models of Zen in the West, we have monks and nuns, married monks (and nuns, although those who use this system tend to call all the ordained "monks"), priests, and laypeople. Many of these people trained in the West are mature practitioners, having undergone the training for decades, and some, perhaps many, are amazingly wise and compassionate teachers.

I think most of us who look honestly at all this see that the training we get in the West produces "journeymen" rather than master teachers. Basically our teachers are practitioners who have at least some minimum preparation to guide others. No doubt the same is true in Asia. Formal training and acknowledgment is only one gate to mastery. Mastery is not, after all, bound by institutions.

Part of the problem is how titles in the West are vastly inflated—and I believe they are in the East as well. However, some who might deserve such titles do appear to be emerging in the West. A few, like Robert Aitken and Shunryu Suzuki, have lived out their full lives. They are not myths, but human beings dealing with real lives. And we can see how over the years insight and personality are integrated. But only time shows this.

So what should we look for as adequate preparation for a teacher? What gives us that journeyman, that one who might become a master? And, frankly, how do we sort out people who may have titles but are probably not prepared to teach at all?

I served for a decade on the membership committee of the American Zen Teachers Association. What we noticed is that people who had solid teaching skills had devoted a great deal of time to sitting. The formation of Zen teachers across traditions, including monastics, priests, and lay teachers, required about a cumulative year of time spent on retreat—something between three and four hundred full days of sitting, eight or nine or ten hours a day, with guidance from teachers during and beyond retreat. This was not the only requirement for membership in the AZTA, but a critical one.

In Zen this intensive training schedule is traditionally experienced through the ninety-day extended monastic retreat, the *ango.* But increasingly it is cultivated through those periods of a week or less, *sesshins,* that accumulate over many years. From my observation, the formation produces different kinds of teachers. But they all are teachers, ordained or lay. I suspect it is this model of decades-long training that will become more normative for the formation of Zen teachers in the West.

I would be wary of any teacher who has not undergone this training, whether through the ninety- or hundred-day retreats or through shorter sesshins over many years. Personally, I think undergoing formal koan introspection training is enormously important as well. This is particularly true for those teachers who have not trained within that extended monastic experience.

However, I wouldn't automatically rule out teachers who have not undergone this preparation. I can think of several teachers I know who were given titles with relatively little training practice. But, through continuing practice, open-hearted investigation, they have become authentic Zen teachers. In other words, I'd be wary but not automatically dismissive of those without that intensive training, either through the monastery or koan curriculum and lots of intensive retreats.

And so, I repeat, titles mean very little. There is no Good Housekeeping Seal of Approval to look for. When looking for a teacher, probably the best thing is to ask people you respect, pretty much what you would do when looking for a lawyer or a doctor. Do some homework.

Here's the bottom line. If you want to practice Zen, find a guide. Ideally this person has some more or less traditional form of authorization, or works closely under the supervision of someone with that authorization. And they should have lots and lots of actual experience with the practice.

Again, it can be very powerful to have a significant monastic experience in one style or another on the Zen Way. And again, completion of formal koan training can be very important. And none of these, nor lack of them, are guarantees, but they are pretty good rules of thumb to follow.

Fortunately, as important as a good teacher is, the practice itself is the most important teacher. Keep your heart open and your eyes equally open; throw yourself into the practice and you'll probably be fine.

# 25

# Of Deserts and Dark Nights

*Midway in the journey of our life*
*I found myself in a dark wood*
—Dante

If we are on a way to awakening, we are awakening from something. That long sleep obviously is something we take comfort in. So waking is going to be a troubling thing. For most of us the first intimations come as some sense of a wrongness in the world. It could be dramatic; something terrible has happened. It could be less so; there is a nagging dissatisfaction with our lives.

This is a powerful moment. Something pulls us in, something calls us to the Way. Poets call it *grace*. Graced with this sense of wrongness, we take up the Way. And, then, if this Way is Zen, we throw ourselves into its disciplines where we quickly find ourselves confronted with some unpleasant truths. There is that noticing how everything passes, which includes our health, our loved ones, and at the last our very lives. There is also a profound challenging of our sense of self. All this, particularly this last point, is a sustained confrontation with the realities of our conditioned existence. What that actually means can be destabilizing.

For some of us, this is more than we can handle. This noticing can exacerbate some psychological disorders. People inclined to disassociation should be careful. People with schizophrenia should be particularly careful. If you have significant psychological concerns, I do believe Zen practice can still be your practice. But it should be undertaken with the full knowledge of and input from competent mental health professionals. I would add, having Zen teachers who have experienced the path over time and have insight beyond the mechanics of the practice is equally important.

Beyond those special concerns, all of us will experience less than pleasant things along this Way. It is a long journey. Actually it is a lifelong journey. And so we will have numerous encounters, go through various states and conditions, discover and forget, wander into byways, and meet wondrous creatures as well the occasional monster. Many, many different things will happen, and among them we will encounter various crises.

Sooner or later there will be a moment when we feel an aridity in our practice. I think of it as an experience of the desert.

In Western mystical traditions it is called *acedia*, originally a Greek word meaning, roughly, "negligence." It looks something like depression, or it can be depression, but it is different; there is a sense of listlessness, a feeling there is nothing to be accomplished.

I recall a time where I heard the Korean monk Seung Sahn give a talk. As is common in Western Zen, after the talk there was a question-and-answer period. Someone asked why is it that people rarely seem to stick with Zen practice. It seems sooner or later most people give up on it. The master smiled broadly, and replied, "Because. Because . . ." We all waited. And then he said, "Because Zen is boring."

Now there is simply laziness. The ancients called this "sloth" and labeled it a sin or a hindrance. The reality is spiritual practice is hard, and many people will simply try it on and discover it is too much. That's real. It happens all the time. Whether it's a sin or not, it is the way things go. But this experience of the desert is about something different.

We take up the Way, and we find we are called to face ourselves. What we find is that we are pretty boring creatures. Our minds return over and over to the same ruts, we appear to have a couple of tape loops we play, over and over again. The favorites tend to be either "I was mistreated" or "I want that so much." There actually aren't a lot of these thoughts, although we can put some interesting twists on them—although not that interesting. The bottom line of it is that we and our stories are all just plain boring. And Zen practice brings us back over and over again to who we are, that boring me, that boring you. No wonder we can feel drained, listless.

The great Christian teacher John of the Cross observes how this listlessness is the curse of the novice. It occurs mostly in the early years of our practice. In our era of instant this and that, please note the word *years*. (If you experience listlessness after weeks or months, you're probably experiencing the laziness mentioned above.) Acedia is something that happens as we dig in, as we actually engage the practice as something important, as we begin to see into what it means.

Writing of acedia, John of the Cross noted how we can "become weary in the more spiritual exercises and flee from them, since these exercises are contrary to sensory satisfaction." He goes on to observe that this arises because we are so used to finding delight in spiritual practices, we become bored when we don't find it.

Here is that issue of boredom again. We want things. For many of us, it's pretty straightforward and outwardly directed. Perhaps we want a car, or a house, or that perfect person. On the spiritual path it isn't all that different. We want bliss. We gain a taste of insight, and if we get it, we want to stay there.

However, as it turns out, all things pass away. Even cars, even bliss, even our moment of insight.

And the experience can be draining. We can become stale. Everything can seem to taste like dust. The Desert Fathers and Mothers had a term for this. These Christian mystics, who lived in the Egyptian deserts during the fourth and fifth centuries, and whose stories and teachings I find endlessly compelling, called it the "noonday demon." That demon is a fiend who took the unaware right in the middle of the day, in the full heat of the desert—when everyone was listless and exhausted.

Aitken Roshi spoke of this experience. He tells of meeting the Jesuit priest and Zen practitioner Thomas Hand. The roshi asked the priest about this problem, common across spiritual disciplines. Aitken Roshi wrote, "He said it was a very important condition, and the person going through that condition must do two things. One is maintain the practice, and the other is to keep in touch with the teacher or spiritual advisor."

We push through and we find new problems.

Here's where we often encounter makyo, experiences of the world taking new shapes. These eruptions of the heart and mind can shift our sense of who we are. The only danger is when we cling to them, thinking they're real and true. It's equally a problem when we push them away. Sometimes they're unpleasant and we don't want to own them, don't want to admit that our minds conjured them up, out of our own thoughts and impulses. It can be embarrassing and distressing. Even so, they, like all things, pass.

And then, like little postcards from the heart, we get various experiences of depth. They might be mixed up with makyo experiences, but not necessarily. These are what the Zen priest Joko Beck called "small intimations." Actually, they often aren't particularly small, but they are confusing. Smaller and larger insights are disruptions and genuine moments of clarity.

When we have these insights, we may find ourselves grasping at them. Buddhist writer and longtime Zen student Barbara O'Brien calls these moments *dukkha nanas*:

A *nana* is a mental phenomenon. It is also used to mean something like "insight knowledge." The early Pali scriptures describe many nanas or insights, pleasant and unpleasant, one passes through on the way to enlightenment. The several *dukkha nanas* are insights into misery, but we can't stop being miserable until we thoroughly understand misery. Passing through a dukkha nana stage is a kind of dark night of the soul.

That dark night of the soul is a reference to the poem by John of the Cross, the Spanish mystic, who described the spiritual path and many of its traps. For me as a Zen Buddhist, the dark night is when everything has finally been revealed as empty and passing. So my work, my life, my spirituality—they're all empty and passing, and this can feel overwhelming. Seeing this, we totter at the edge of despair—and if we are not careful it is possible to tumble into the abyss.

I recall when I first passed the Source of Mu koan. At the time, as I responded "correctly," I felt a wave of despair. *This* is it? This is all there is to it? It was my tumble into a dark night. The dark night might bring us to a new corner of that desert. We may have thought it all dry and parched before, but this becomes a new hell. The heat is more fierce, but it is no longer in the noonday.

Instead we are cast into the depths of darkness. This does not include visions and voices, or the more common distortions of makyo. If they recur, it is in a way that is distressing or misleading. They're just like gnats buzzing around.

However, this is the darkness of emptiness. This, for me, was my first experience of the place the Source of Mu took me. There is a danger of experiencing it as blankness, a dead emptiness. It isn't uncommon—and it can even persist. I think of the koan of the young woman and the monk. She leaned into him and asked him what he felt. He responded he was like a dead branch, nothing but cold ashes. That is the kind of emptiness we can experience in the dark night of the soul. It can be a type of despair. And there is an enormous danger here.

The Zen teacher Ruben Habito, who was for many years a Jesuit priest, writes of this tremulous moment:

> If we find ourselves in such a dark night of the soul, the Psalmist invites us: let us not try to find some way of turning our attention away from the darkness and the pain, or to seek some kind of false consolation or diversion.
>
> We are invited not to succumb to the different weapons of mass distraction that our society provides for us, seeking momentary pleasures, burying ourselves in our work or even in our studies, taking up some mindless computer game that will ease away the pain or anxiety or turmoil we feel coming from within. Instead, we are invited to be still, and stay there in that darkness, and wait, and trust.

To shift to another koan image, we must be willing to step away from the top of the one-hundred-foot pole; we must let go even of emptiness. As our teacher Hakuin commented on the dead branch, if that young woman leaned into him, green shoots would appear. We need to pass through the dark desert; we need to continue on. Here we find ourselves passing from doubt into the Great Doubt.

And from the Great Doubt, well, we will find the Great Awakening.

# 26

# As Intimate As a Kiss

HOW DOES ALL THIS come together? What does living the Zen Way look like? What is it like to explore the koan of our lives among those who speak this language of dragons fluently? A key to the treasure house, to the point of our lives, of living fully with some grace and joy, is finding an authentic spiritual discipline. A classic koan points to the truth of this.

This encounter, between Changsha and the temple director, is found in case 36 of the *Blue Cliff Record*. It invites us into the dance, inviting us to learn when to pay attention, when to lead, when to follow, and, just as important, when to sit this one out.

One day Changsha went off to wander in the mountains. When he returned, the temple director met him at the gate and asked, "So where have you been?"

Changsha replied, "I've been strolling about in the hills."

"Which way did you go?"

"I went out following the scented grasses and came back chasing the falling flowers."

The director smiled. "That's exactly the feeling of spring."

Changsha, agreed, adding, "It's better than autumn dew falling on lotuses."

The *Blue Cliff Record* had several editors. Xuedou was the first, gathering the one hundred stories of the *Blue Cliff Record* sometime in the eleventh century, and adding a word or two of his own by way of comment. Xuedou's comments are usually pithy and often cut through right to the heart of the matter.

In fact, as this particular case is published, it includes a little coda from Xuedou. After Changsha's description of following scented grasses and falling flowers, and the director's appreciation, and Changsha's pointed conclusion, Xuedou adds his own: "I'm grateful for this answer."

Me too. It points us on with a gentle hand. More than most stories from the world's treasure trove of spiritual teachings, this story of spring flowers and autumn dew points directly to the secret of our path. What is the secret that finds the heart of a spiritual life in noticing the turning of spring to summer— of picnics and walks in the woods? A rereading of Henry

Thoreau's *Walden* might be interesting, but this anecdote has all we need.

First, "I went out following the scented grasses." Everything is in flower, as those among us with allergies can attest. The world is alive. We are alive. Notice it. Feel it. Throw yourselves into the moment. Not some other moment—this one. For Changsha, it's a walk in the countryside.

But then the line about the autumn dew: "It's better than autumn dew falling on lotuses." We're invited into the cosmic play, found as flashes of insight throughout our lives but most commonly noticed when we're quiet.

It is our intimation of interconnections so vast, so very vast that you and I—indeed everything we can name—collapses, like a star pulled into a black hole. Even words like "interconnected web," or my preferred term, "boundless," slightly miss the point.

Perhaps you've had that taste of reality in all its vastness. It's a gift of our humanity, encountered by rich and poor, by educated and ignorant. Now and then we all catch a moment of its truth, like a flash of lightning in a summer storm. Or maybe it just haunts an occasional dream.

The deep connections that our tradition sings of, the perspective we are all woven together, so finely that we can't even find our separateness, is an important encounter. I would even call it the God beyond God. But again the words fail. For those of us who've noticed this experience, we might recognize that description of autumn dew falling on a lotus.

And it is important to notice this experience, however we name it. It ties us together and puts the lie of our separateness and sense of isolation to rest. But Changsha adds something. We don't live there. Or more importantly, we find that vastness nowhere but in things—not things in general, but specific things. The person sitting next to you reveals that whole. Your own experience of this moment manifests the universe itself and the space beyond naming. The whole interdependent web is revealed in a single flower.

Changsha calls us to the world, of the precious individual, of scented flowers. Here we're invited to see how that boundless place, that black hole of all ideas and separateness, is also this place. Everything is tied up together in some great cosmic play that is so vast our words fail to convey it. But it is also nothing other than you and me.

Here's the deal. We spend a little time noticing, and then the time comes again to act. And don't worry, it will. When that time comes, well, we might even notice whether the dance is calling us to lead, to follow, or to sit this one out. We gain a perspective that even deserves the word *holy*.

Not fully clear? Well, there's another story about Changsha

from many years before. Perhaps it can underscore our invitation. He's sitting on the side of a hill with an old friend. It's late evening and they're looking up at the moon. The presence of the moon in these stories is another pointer to the "great big," to that sense of the divine, of the holy, of the vast unnamable, of the interdependent web.

Out of their shared silence, contemplating the beauty of it all, Changsha's companion says, "That's the secret. Right there. Right here." He pauses, and adds, "Too bad people don't know how to use it."

We're being invited into something. It isn't rocket science, but it is the hidden secret of our lives. How do we act with grace in this world? How do we do the work that our lives call us to? How are we decent parents, loving partners, good friends? Well, all is revealed in a moment when two friends sit on a hillside gazing up at the full moon.

Changsha replies, "I'll show you how to use it." And with that he pushes his friend over on his side.

I suspect there was laughter. Forget the high falutin' theory, forget the philosophy. For right now, just this moment.

One of my favorite cartoonists over the years was Gary Larson. Seriously weird, he penned a strip called "The Far Side." In one strip there's a cow guru and a cow disciple. The cow guru says to the cow disciple, "Don't forget to stop and eat the roses."

Some platitudes are platitudes, repeated over and over again, because they're true. Stop to smell the roses. Well, unless you're a cow. And then you have your own instructions as well.

Just open your heart to what is going on. The autumn dew is always with us, the full moon is never very far away. Notice the clear clean moments as they present, but our invitation for this summer is to be present, to wander out following the scented grasses.

We'll find it all in the scented grasses.

# 27

# The Last Koan

THERE IS one last koan according to the Zen scholar and priest Victor Sogen Hori. It is passed on to the student at the end of formal monastic training and is carried away without any immediate expectation of a response. It is like the huatou, the case that can be examined endlessly, and for which an endless number of responses can be found.

Professor Hori gives us examples: "Sum up all the *Record of Linji* in one phrase," and Hakuin's "not yet."

Professor Hori points out that, even at the end of training, what we have cultivated is simply a "sacred fetus" (which I also like for its Daoist sensibility, a hint of our multiple ancestry). There is much more to do, much more to develop. I suggest it is also a reminder that we never cease training. However skillfully we have delved into the Great Matter, as the old Zen saying goes, "Shakyamuni is still practicing."

Here, again, I find myself thinking of the oxherding pictures, that wonderful map of awakening that evolved over the ages in China. The last of them takes place after the Great Emptiness, after a pure experience of nature, and it presents a fat old man walking into the village with "bliss-bestowing hands." For me, that is the expression of the last koan: Ordinary, ordinary.

Another way of looking at it, all of it, from beginning to end, is expressed completely by Master Dogen, in his fascicle "Genjokoan," translated by Robert Aitken and Kaz Tanahashi.

As all things are Buddhadharma, there is delusion and realization, practice, and birth and death, and there are buddhas and sentient beings. As the myriad things are without an abiding self, there is no delusion, no realization, no buddha, no sentient being, no birth and death. The Buddha Way is, basically, leaping clear of the many and the one; thus there is birth and death, delusion and realization, sentient beings and buddhas. Yet in attachment, blossoms fall, and in aversion, weeds spread. To carry yourself forward and experience myriad things is delusion. That myriad things come forth and experience themselves is awakening. Those who have great realization of delusion are buddhas; those who are greatly deluded about realization are sentient beings. Further, there are those who continue realizing beyond realization, who are in delusion throughout delusion. When buddhas are truly buddhas they do not necessarily notice that they are buddhas. However, they are actualized buddhas, who go on actualizing buddhas.

Actualized buddhas going on actualizing buddhas beyond all knowing—this is nothing other than the heart of true entrusting in action. Elsewhere in the Shobogenzo, Dogen tells us, "You attain the marrow and are inevitably transmitted the Dharma through your utmost sincerity and your trusting heart. There is no path that comes from anything other than sincere trust."

All things have become one, even as they are separate. Knowing this, at some times more clearly, at others less so, we proceed into the sacred ordinariness of our lives.

As intimate as a kiss. As intimate as a breath.

Only just this.

# APPENDIX

# *The Five Styles—*
# *Some Example Koans*

Chapter 22 discussed Hakuin's typology of five styles of koan and cited two examples for each. Here are the texts of those koans.

### *Hosshin or Dharmakaya Koans,*
### *the Koans of Nonduality*

*Gateless Gate, Case 1:* A student of the Way asked Zhaozhou, "Does a dog have Buddha nature?" Zhaozhou replied, "Mu" ("No").

*Sound of the Single Hand:* Master Hakuin said, "We all know the sound of two hands clapping. What is the sound of the single hand?"

## *Kikan, the Koans of Action Arising Out of the Empty*

*Gateless Gate, Case 14:* The teacher Nanchuan came upon the monks of the eastern and western halls arguing over a cat. He took the cat and held it up with one hand, holding a knife in the other. He said, "Anyone! If you can say a word, I will spare this cat. If you cannot, I will kill it." No one spoke, so Nanchuan cut the cat in two. That evening when Zhaozhou returned to the monastery, Nanchuan told him what had happened. Zhaozhou removed a sandal from his foot, balanced it on his head, and walked out of the meeting. Nanchuan muttered, "If only he had been there, the cat would have lived."

*Gateless Gate, Case 37:* A student of the Way asked Zhaozhou, "What is the meaning of Bodhidharma coming from the west?" Zhaozhou responded, "The oak tree in the courtyard."

## *Gonsen, the Koans of Skillful Use of Words*

*Blue Cliff Record, Case 6:* Yunmen asked his assembly, "I don't ask you about before the fifteenth of the month. Say something about after the fifteenth." When no one responded, he said, "Every day is a good day."

*Gateless Gate, Case 7:* A student of the Way asks Zhaozhou, "I've just come to the monastery. Please, guide me." Zhaozhou responds, "Have you eaten yet?" The student replies, "Yes, sir." Zhaozhou says, "Wash your bowls." The student awakened.

## Nanto, or Difficult Koans

*Gateless Gate, Case 38:* Wuzu said, "It is like an ox who passes through a latticed window. Its horns, its four legs, all pass through." Then he asked, "Why can't its tail pass through?"

*Entangling Vines, Case 162:* An old woman supported a monk in a hermitage on her property for twenty years. She had a young girl take him a meal every day. Then one day she told the girl to give him a hug and ask, "What do you feel right now?" She did and reported back the hermit responded, "An old tree on a cold cliff / midwinter—no warmth at all." The woman exclaimed, "For twenty years I've housed and fed that fraud." And with that she drove the hermit away and then burned down his hermitage.

# Acknowledgments

Elements of this book have seen print before as partially developed thoughts. Some appeared in my previous books, others in my blog Monkey Mind, others as articles in various magazines. Some even in sermons delivered at Unitarian Universalist churches. I'm grateful for the opportunity to further reflect and expand on these recurring themes in my life and what I see as themes in the lives of many others.

There are so many people to thank for help along the way, too many to completely list here, but still, some names must be said.

Of course at the heart of the matter are my various official and nearly official teachers, including my first Zen teachers Shunryu Suzuki and Mel Sojun Weitsman; my ordination master Houn Jiyu Kennett; Myozen Delport, who guided my meditation practice into new depths; Jim Wilson, who introduced me to koan introspection; and most of all to John Tarrant, who guided me to the depths of koan introspection; my Dharma siblings David Weinstein, Joan Sutherland, and Daniel

Terragno, who helped, pushed, and sometimes dragged me in many different ways along the path.

I particularly owe a great and continuing debt to my fellow teachers at the Boundless Way Zen project, especially Melissa Myozen Blacker, David DaeAn Rynick, and Josh Jiun Bartok, who did double duty as my editor at Wisdom Publications.

And endless thanks to those who have read parts or even all of this manuscript at one stage of its writing or another, and whose comments allowed me to avoid several traps: Florence Caplow, James Cordova, Mary Gates, Desmond Gilna, Gesshin Greenwood, Genjo Marinello, Dana Miller, Wendy Egyoku Nakao, Edward Oberholtzer, Pat Enkyo O'Hara, Douglas Philips, Dosho Port, Dave Rutschman, Seisen Saunders, Jan Seymour-Ford, Henry Shukman, Stephen Slottow, Dana Veldon, J. Thomas Wardle, Jay Rinsen Weik, Mo Weinhart, and Tetsugan Zummach.

What is useful within these pages owes a great deal to all these people, maybe everything. The mistakes, sadly, are all mine. Some, I have to admit, were made in the face of strong counsel otherwise.

# Bibliography

Aitken, Robert, trans. with commentary. *The Gateless Barrier: The Wu-Men Kuan (Mumonkan)*. San Francisco: North Point Press, 1990.

————. *Mind of Clover: Essays in Zen Buddhist Ethics*. San Francisco: North Point Press, 1984.

————. *Taking the Path of Zen*. San Francisco: North Point Press, 1982.

Anderson, Reb. *Being Upright: Zen Meditation and the Bodhisattva Precepts*. Berkeley, CA: Rodmell Press, 2001.

Austin, James. *Zen and the Brain: Toward an Understanding of Meditation and Consciousness*. Cambridge, MA: MIT Press, 1998.

Batchelor, Stephen. *Confessions of a Buddhist Atheist*. New York: Spiegel & Grau, 2010.

Bayda, Ezra. *Being Zen: Bringing Meditation to Life*. Boston: Shambhala Publications, 2002.

Bielefeldt, Carl. *Dogen's Manuals of Zen Meditation*. Berkeley, CA: University of California Press, 1988.

Bodiford, William M. *Soto Zen in Medieval Japan*. Honolulu: Kuroda Institute, University of Hawaii Press, 1993.

Boshan. *Great Doubt: Practicing Zen in the World*. Translated and introduced by Jeff Shore. Somerville, MA: Wisdom Publications, 2016.

Broughton, Jeffrey L., and Elise Yoko Watanabe, trans. *The Chan Whip*

*Anthology: A Companion to Zen Practice.* Oxford: Oxford University Press, 2014.

Buksbazen, John Daishin. *Zen Meditation in Plain English.* Somerville, MA: Wisdom Publications, 2002.

Buswell, Robert, Jr. *The Zen Monastic Experience.* Princeton, NJ: Princeton University Press, 1993.

Caplow, Florence, and Susan Moon. *The Hidden Lamp: Stories from Twenty-Five Centuries of Awakened Women.* Somerville, MA: Wisdom Publications, 2013.

Cleary, Thomas, trans. *Book of Serenity.* Hudson, NY: Lindisfarne Press, 1990.

————, trans. *Secrets of the Blue Cliff Record: Zen Comments by Hakuin and Tenkei.* Boston: Shambhala Publications, 2000.

Cleary, Thomas, and J. C. Cleary, trans. *The Blue Cliff Record.* Boston: Shambhala Publications, 1992.

Cook, Francis H., trans. *The Record of Transmitting the Light: Zen Master Keizan's Denkoroku.* Los Angeles: Center Publications, 1991.

Dogen, Eihei. *Moon in a Dewdrop: Writings of Zen Master Dogen.* Edited by Kazuaki Tanahashi. San Francisco: North Point Press, 1985.

Dumoulin, Heinrich. *Zen Buddhism: A History.* 2 vols. New York: Macmillan Publishing, 1988, 1990.

Ferguson, Andy. *Zen's Chinese Heritage: The Masters and Their Teachings.* Somerville, MA: Wisdom Publications, 2011.

Ford, James. *If You're Lucky, Your Heart Will Break.* Somerville, MA: Wisdom Publications, 2012.

————. *Zen Master WHO? A Guide to the People and Stories of Zen.* Somerville, MA: Wisdom Publications, 2006.

Ford, James Ishmael, and Melissa Myozen Blacker. *The Book of Mu:*

*Essential Writings on Zen's Most Important Koan.* Somerville, MA: Wisdom Publications, 2011.

Gu, Guo. *Passing Through the Gateless Barrier: Koan Practice for Real Life.* Boulder, CO: Shambhala Publications, 2016.

Habito, Ruben. *Living Zen, Loving God.* Somerville, MA: Wisdom Publications, 1995.

Hakuin Ekaku. *Hakuin's Precious Mirror Cave: A Zen Miscellany.* Translated by Norman Waddell. Berkeley, CA: Counterpoint, 2009.

———.*Wild Ivy: The Spiritual Autobiography of Zen Master Hakuin.* Translated by Norman Waddell. Boston: Shambhala Publications, 1999.

———. *Zen Words for the Heart: Hakuin's Commentary on the Heart Sutra.* Translated by Norman Waddell. Boston: Shambhala Publications, 1996.

Heine, Steven. *Dogen and the Koan Tradition: A Tale of Two Shobogenzo Texts.* Albany, NY: State University of New York Press, 1994.

Heine, Steven, and Dale S. Wright, eds. *The Koan: Texts and Contexts in Zen Buddhism.* Oxford: Oxford University Press, 2000.

Hori, Victor. *Zen Sand: The Book of Capping Phrases for Koan Practice.* Honolulu, HI: University of Hawai'i Press, 2003.

Jaffe, Richard. *Neither Monk Nor Layman: Clerical Marriage in Modern Japanese Buddhism.* Princeton, NJ: Princeton University Press, 2002.

Kapleau, Philip. *The Three Pillars of Zen: Teaching, Practice, and Enlightenment.* Tokyo: Weatherhill, 1965.

Kennett, Jiyu. *Zen Is Eternal Life.* Emeryville, CA: Dharma Publishing, 1976.

Kirchner, Thomas Yuho, trans. and annotator. *Entangling Vines: A Classic Collection of Zen Koans.* Somerville, MA: Wisdom Publications, 2013.

Larson, Gary. *The Complete Far Side.* Kansas City, MO: Andrews McMeel Publishing, 2014.

Leggett, Trevor. *The Warrior Koans: Early Zen in Japan.* London: Arkana, 1985.

Leighton, Taigen Daniel, with Yi Wu, trans. *Cultivating the Empty Field: The Silent Illumination of Zen Master Hongzhi.* San Francisco: North Point Press, 1991.

———. *Just This Is It: Dongshan and the Practice of Suchness.* Boston: Shambhala Publications, 2015.

Loori, John Daido, ed. *The Art of Just Sitting: Essential Writings on the Zen Practice of Shikantaza.* Boston: Shambhala Publications, 2002.

———. *The Heart of Being: Moral and Ethical Teachings of Zen Buddhism.* Boston: Charles Tuttle, 1996.

———, ed. *Sitting with Koans: Essential Writings on the Practice of Zen Koan Introspection.* Boston: Shambhala Publications, 2006.

Macinnes, Elaine. *The Flowing Bridge: Guidance on Beginning Zen Koans.* Somerville, MA: Wisdom Publications, 2007.

Maezumi, Taizan, and Bernie Glassman. *On Zen Practice: Body, Breath & Mind.* Boston: Wisdom Publications, 2001.

Magid, Barry. *Nothing Is Hidden: The Psychology of Zen Koans.* Somerville, MA: Wisdom Publications, 2013.

———. *Ordinary Mind: Exploring the Common Ground of Zen and Psychotherapy.* Somerville, MA: Wisdom Publications, 2005.

McRae, John R. *Seeing Through Zen: Encounter, Transformation and Genealogy in Chinese Chan Buddhism.* Berkeley, CA: University of California Press, 2003.

Miura, Isshu, and Ruth Fuller Sasaki. *Zen Dust: The History of the Koan and Koan Study in Rinzai (Lin-chi) Zen.* New York: Harcourt, Brace & World, 1966.

Rizzetto, Diane Eshin. *Waking Up to What You Do: A Zen Practice for*

*Meeting Every Situation with Intelligence and Compassion.* Boston: Shambhala Publications, 2005.

Sekida, Katsuki. *Zen Training: Methods and Philosophy.* New York: Weatherhill, 1975.

Seung Sahn. *Only Don't Know: The Teaching Letters of Zen Master Seung Sahn.* San Francisco: Four Seasons Foundation, 1982.

———. *Ten Gates: The Kong-an Teaching of Zen Master Seung Sahn.* Boston: Shambhala Publications, 2007.

Sheng Yen. *The Method of No-Method: The Chan Practice of Silent Illumination.* Boston: Shambhala Publications, 2008.

———. *Shattering the Great Doubt: The Chan Practice of Huatou.* Boston: Shambhala Publications, 2009.

Shibayama, Zenkei. *Zen Comments on the Mumonkan: The Authoritative Translation, with Commentary, of a Basic Zen Text.* San Francisco: Harper & Row, 1984.

Shrobe, Richard. *Elegant Failure: A Guide to Zen Koans.* Berkeley, CA: Rodmell Press, 2010.

Suzuki, Shunryu. *Zen Mind, Beginner's Mind.* Boston: Shambhala Publications, 2010.

Ta Hui. *Swampland Flowers: The Letters and Lectures of Zen Master Ta Hui.* Translated by J. C. Cleary. Boston: Shambhala Publications, 2006.

Tarrant, John. *Bring Me the Rhinoceros: And Other Zen Koans to Bring You Joy.* New York: Harmony Books, 2004.

———. *Light Inside the Dark: Zen, Soul, and the Spiritual Life.* New York: HarperCollins Publishers, 1998.

Uchiyama, Kosho. *Opening the Hand of Thought: Approach to Zen.* New York: Arkana, 1993.

Underhill, Evelyn. *Mysticism: A Study in the Nature and Development of Man's Spiritual Consciousness.* London: Methuen & Co. Ltd, 1967 (reprint, original 1911).

Wick, Gerry Shishin. *The Book of Equanimity: Illuminating Classic Zen Koans.* Somerville, MA: Wisdom Publications, 2005.

Yamada, Koun, trans. with commentary. *Gateless Gate.* Tucson, AZ: University of Arizona Press, 1979.

———. *Zen: The Authentic Gate.* Somerville, MA: Wisdom Publications, 2015.

Warner, Brad. *Hardcore Zen: Punk Rock, Monster Movies & the Truth about Reality.* Somerville, MA: Wisdom Publications, 2003.

Yampolsky, Philip B., trans. *The Platform Sutra of the Sixth Patriarch.* New York: Columbia University Press, 1967.

# Index

# About the Author

JAMES ISHMAEL FORD, Roshi, has been a Zen practitioner for nearly fifty years. He is ordained both as a Soto Zen Buddhist priest and as a koan teacher in the Harada-Yasutani tradition. He served on the membership committee of the American Zen Teachers Association for ten years, and a three-year term on the Board of Directors of the Soto Zen Buddhist Association. James was a founding member of Boundless Way Zen and served as its first abbot. Today he guides Zen sanghas in Long Beach and

Costa Mesa, California, and Seattle, Washington. His personal webpage is at http://www.jamesishmaelford.com.

He is also an ordained Unitarian Universalist minister. He is minister-emeritus of the First Unitarian Church of Providence, in Rhode Island. And he is currently affiliated as a community minister with the Unitarian Universalist Church of Long Beach, in California.

He is the author or editor of five books, mostly addressing aspects of Zen history and practice, as well as articles for *Buddhadharma, Lion's Roar, Tricycle,* and the *Unitarian Universalist World*. He blogs as Monkey Mind, which is hosted by the religion portal Patheos. He lives with his spouse, Jan Seymour-Ford, in Long Beach, California.

# What to Read Next
# from Wisdom Publications

IF YOU'RE LUCKY, YOUR HEART WILL BREAK
*Field Notes from a Zen Life*
James Ishmael Ford

"A valuable companion filled with encouragement for beginners and experienced meditators alike."—Diane Eshin Rizzetto, author of *Waking Up to What You Do*

ENTANGLING VINES
*A Classic Collection of Zen Koans*
Thomas Yuhō Kirchner
Foreword by Nelson Foster

"A masterpiece. It will be our inspiration for 10,000 years."
—Robert Aitken, author of *Taking the Path of Zen*

THE CROW FLIES BACKWARDS
*And Other New Zen Koans*
Ross Bolleter

A uniquely modern take on Zen koans—like nothing you've seen before.

ZEN MASTER RAVEN
*The Teachings of a Wise Old Bird*
Robert Aitken
Foreword by Nelson Foster

"A new koan anthology that reflects the distinct flavor of American Zen Buddhist practice. This is a beautiful and worthy final teaching from Aitken."—*Publishers Weekly*

SITTING WITH KOANS
*Essential Writings on Zen Koan Introspection*
Edited by John Daido Loori
With an introduction by Thomas Yuhō Kirchner

"Required reading for those interested in how koans are used in Zen practice."—*Shambhala Sun*

# About Wisdom Publications

Wisdom Publications is the leading publisher of classic and contemporary Buddhist books and practical works on mindfulness. To learn more about us or to explore our other books, please visit our website at wisdompubs.org or contact us at the address below.

Wisdom Publications
199 Elm Street
Somerville, MA 02144 USA

We are a 501(c)(3) organization, and donations in support of our mission are tax deductible.

Wisdom Publications is affiliated with the Foundation for the Preservation of the Mahayana Tradition (FPMT).